Get

C000182076

Preaching
the Cross

Nigel Styles

PT RESOURCES

CHRISTIAN
FOCUS

Scripture quotations are from *The Holy Bible, English Standard Version*, copyright © 2001 by Crossway Bibles, a publishing ministry of Good News Publishers. Used by permission. All rights reserved. ESV Text Edition: 2011.

Scripture quotations marked 'NLT' are taken from *The Holy Bible, New Living Translation*, copyright © 1996. Used by permission of Tyndale House Publishers, Inc., Wheaton, Illinois 60189. All rights reserved.

Copyright © Proclamation Trust

paperback ISBN 978-1-5271-0384-9
epub ISBN 978-1-5271-0433-4
mobi ISBN 978-1-5271-0434-1

10 9 8 7 6 5 4 3 2 1

Published in 2019
by
Christian Focus Publications Ltd.,
Geanies House, Fearn, Ross-shire,
IV20 1TW, Great Britain
with
Proclamation Trust Resources,
Willcox House, 140-148 Borough High Street,
London, SE1 1LB, England, Great Britain.
www.proctrust.org.uk

www.christianfocus.com

Cover design by Tom Barnard
Printed in Malta

CONTENTS

SERIES PREFACE

In 1592, the Puritan William Perkins published a tract on preaching that he called 'The Art of Prophesying'. He recognised that 'the preparation of sermons is an everyday task in the church, but it is still a tremendous responsibility and by no means easy. In fact it is doubtful if there is a more difficult challenge in the theological disciplines than that of homiletics .'

Since its beginnings in the summer of 1981, the Proclamation Trust has been committed to helping preachers in that tremendous – and difficult – responsibility. We believe that the Bible is God's written Word and that, by the work of the Holy Spirit, as it is faithfully preached, God's voice is truly heard. With Perkins, we are confident that through the preaching of the Word 'those who hear are called into the state of grace, and preserved in it'.

This series of short books is designed to help preachers in that 'everyday task'. Experienced practitioners share their wisdom, gained after years of 'toil, struggling with all his energy that he powerfully works within [us]' (Col. 1:28-29).

We hope that these short books will help all of us to progress in our understanding of the task in hand; to set the novice preacher on a course of faithful preaching; to hone the skills of the experienced preacher; to help preaching groups sharpen one another.

However you use this book we hope that it will achieve its twin aims. That you would <u>get</u> preaching (understanding the task at hand), and get <u>preaching</u> (doing more preaching). May God use these books to renew a commitment in all of us to preach the Word (2 Tim. 4:2).

Jon Gemmell & Nigel Styles
Series Editors

Introduction

I am convinced that Christians must preach the cross.

Indeed, preaching the cross is central for our mission to the world. It is hard to think of a better first volume in this series of books about preaching. Let's begin with the really big thing: let's get preaching the cross.

I need to warn you at the very start that this book has a long run up, especially considering its modest overall size. Before we get to the actual subject of 'preaching the cross', there are three chapters of initial groundwork. We need to be clear what we mean by 'preaching' and what we mean by 'the cross'. We also need to clarify why words are so important. Only then will we be in a position to consider our subject of 'preaching the cross'.

May this book strengthen us in broadcasting the seemingly foolish message of the cross.

Nigel Styles
Cornhill Training Course, London, 2019

1
PREACHING THE CROSS

Since being appointed to my role as Director of the Cornhill Training Course in Spring 2016, and in preparation for writing this book, I have read some twenty to thirty books about preaching. Forty years ago, there simply wasn't that quantity of good, contemporary books to instruct us and sustain us in the task of preaching. Now, there are many in circulation and more coming off the printing press every year.

In my reading, I have realised that most of these books assume – and some positively argue for – a particular view of preaching.

The first widespread idea is that the word 'preaching' means 'giving sermons'. So the phrase 'preaching the cross' is roughly equivalent to 'giving sermons about the cross'. Perhaps most of us share that assumption. In the wake of such a notion may come a whole host of other expectations about the shape of a sermon (usually three points with alliterating headings), its style (perhaps caricatured as 'oral commentary'), its curriculum (usually sequential preaching through Bible books) and its length (specified by the conventions of our particular congregation). That's the assumption about the 'what' of preaching.

The second assumption concerns the 'where'. Such sermons are given 'to the church congregation, gathered (usually) on a Sunday'. They will normally happen in the place where our church meets each week, which might be a church building, or a hired school or community hall, or any one of a myriad of other possibilities ... but the home of preaching is the pulpit, lectern or stage at the front of the venue where our church normally meets, and from which the Sunday sermon is preached.

The majority of those listening will therefore be converted, usually church members only (or just a random small group of them who happen to be in attendance on any given week). Perhaps there may be some non-Christians there, but only in a tiny minority because if they were present in significant numbers, then the sermon would stop being 'preaching' and become 'evangelism'.

The third assumption is about the 'who' that preaches such sermons. Because they are done in the main Sunday gathering of a church, presumably the authorised church pastor-teacher or leader (or their assistant, or an occasional preacher, or someone invited by them) will normally be the person to give these sermons.

But are these assumptions right? When we talk about 'preaching the cross' how much of this mindset is appropriate? Are we really talking about the recognised church leader giving sermons about the cross to the Christian gathering? That's the question we are going to explore in this chapter.

'Preaching' vocabulary in the New Testament

Let's first consider what 'preaching' is.

This table lists three of the Greek verbs most frequently used in the New Testament for 'preaching'. There are more verbs used than just these three, but these are the most common.

Greek word	meaning	occurrence
euangelizomai	bring good news announce good news proclaim the gospel	54
katangello	proclaim announce	18
kerysso	announce make known proclaim aloud make proclamation as a herald	59

In contrast to the view that 'preaching' is something that happens primarily in the context of the church family, in the vast majority of cases where these words are used, they refer to something like pioneer evangelism, preaching to unbelievers.

The first word euangelizomai describes something that is done generally in a public context, and where the content is the gospel message (or some particular aspect of it).

There are two occasions where this 'evangelising' seems to be to believers (rather than to non-Christians) – in Luke 1:19, where Gabriel brings the good news of John the Baptist's ministry, and in Romans 1:15 where Paul wants to preach the gospel to the Christians in Rome. But even these two uses are with an eye on the wider world (for John will turn the world back to God in repentance, and Paul wants to enlist the support of the Roman church for his mission to Spain). And there is one occurrence where 'good news' is definitely proclaimed to a Christian, as Timothy 'brings the good news' to Paul that the Thessalonians are 'standing firm' as Christians (1 Thess. 3:6).

Apart from these three (possible) exceptions, the direction of travel is clear: *euangelizomai* is about the proclamation of the gospel to the world. It is certainly not restricted to Christian gatherings. It happens to shepherds on the hillside above Bethlehem, in the region around Jordan amongst those listening to John, in a hostile synagogue in Nazareth, in cities and villages and 'other towns', in the temple and from house to house. It happens with an Ethiopian eunuch, to 'all the towns' a Christian traveller passes through, in place after place Paul journeyed, and all the way to Rome. It happens in Corinth, in Galatia, in Rome, and in the lands beyond Corinth, in any place where Christ had not already been named. And on and on.

Katangello follows a similar pattern: the context is public and the content is Christ and the gospel. Again, there are just a couple of exceptions: in Romans 1:8, the proclamation is of the Roman Christians' faith in all the world, and in 1 Corinthians 11:26, the proclamation of the Lord's death is 'as often as you eat this bread and drink this cup', so that, as the Protestant Reformers claimed, the sacraments communicate the same gospel and promises as the written word, but in a different form, as 'visible words'. But two such exceptions test and prove the validity of the general rule: Christ and the gospel is publicly proclaimed.

Kerysso is perhaps best paraphrased as an 'announcing' since the word carries <u>both</u> the idea of the act of the announcing <u>and</u> the content of what is announced. 'In the vast majority of these instances, the context of the proclamation is a public one ... almost uniformly, the substance of the message proclaimed where *kerysso* is used is the gospel message and its implications (or, more broadly, the teaching of or about Jesus)'[1].

Surveying all these 131 occasions of 'preaching', I am not persuaded that <u>any</u> of them can be securely tied, uniquely to the Christian assembly, as we might assume. In fact, it would seem that New Testament preaching finds its natural context in the unbelieving world. Preaching is what you do to proclaim the good news of the Lord Jesus Christ to nations in darkness. That is not a reason to abandon preaching within the Christian assembly, but there seems little evidence that it is to be <u>particularly</u> in church.

---

1   Jonathan Griffiths: *Preaching in the New Testament* (IVP, 2017) p. 32.

'Preaching' examples in the New Testament

Let's zoom into a specific example, and examine the 'preaching' of the Apostle Paul. What did he think he was doing when he preached?

In 1 Corinthians 2:1-5, Paul is discussing his evangelizing visit to Corinth in Acts 18. This is the third of three paragraphs making a similar point that, when he visited, the message that Paul preached (1:18-25), the church that resulted (1:26-31) and the method he used as a preacher (2:1-5) are all outwardly unimpressive.

The background is significant here: public speakers of the day were verbal showmen, with impressive, spell-binding oratory. They were preachers with a capital 'P'! If a new speaker came to town, a crowd would gather waiting to be impressed. A persuasive speaker could expect to be adopted by a wealthy patron, climbing up the social ladder and into political power. As time went on, public speaking developed into an end in itself, merely trying to please the crowd, but without serious content or intent. The goal was applause, the motive vanity and the casualty truth.

In sharp contrast to that contemporary setting in Corinth ...

Paul was not an impressive speaker (1a, 3-4a)

Because Paul has had such influence on the world for 2,000 years, we find it difficult to believe that his audiences did not consider him impressive. When judged by what was revered in his day, Paul came across as nervous and rather shaky. In 2 Corinthians, where Paul is dealing with a group regarded as the 'super-apostles', he refers to their criticism of him: they thought that he was nothing much to look at, and nothing much to listen to (2 Cor. 10:10). His preaching was neither 'plausible' (1 Cor. 2:4, that is, 'persuasive') nor 'words of wisdom' (4, in other words 'matching contemporary rhetorical expectations').

Paul had renounced 'impressiveness' deliberately (1-2a, 4b)

When Paul came to Corinth he decided (2) to renounce self-reliance in order to emphasise the weak-seeming cross. 'Decided' implies a deliberate turning aside from the methods of the rhetoricians. Instead, Paul's single focus and passion would be the gospel of the crucified Messiah, and that is because the power of God is in that gospel (cf 1:18). What Paul is looking for is not the 'proof' which comes from the crowd's applause, but what is observable as the Spirit powerfully saves individuals, and changes human lives.

Why Paul did this (5)

Just as the church should boast of nothing in themselves but only in the God of the gospel (1:29-31), so the goal of the true gospel preacher is that his hearers trust that same God, alone and completely. How easy it would have been for the Corinthians to put their trust in the latest impressive speaker. But God's power isn't to be found in any preacher, but only in His gospel (1:18).

With that context in mind, let's examine what this passage tells us that Paul did during his time in Corinth. Clearly his visit was all about words. One of our key 'proclamation' words (*katangello*) is used in 1 Corinthians 2:1. Paul wanted to distance himself from other public speakers who were also using words, but Paul's response is not that he did not proclaim at all, but that his proclamation was of a particular type: he decided not to use the tricks of their rhetorical trade ('lofty speech or wisdom'), but instead to have a single-minded focus on 'Jesus Christ and him crucified'. All else was put to one side. Paul employed no verbal fireworks, but straightforwardly proclaimed Jesus and His death alone.

Paul's own summary of his visit to Corinth is that he came to 'proclaim'. Let's compare Paul's description here with how Luke-the-author-of-Acts describes that same preaching in Acts 18.

These are the verbs that Luke uses to describe what Paul did (with their dictionary definitions to explain some nuance of meaning):

1	reasoned (Acts 18:4)	discuss, hold a debate
2	tried to persuade (4)	try to convince
3	occupied with the word (5)	hold fast, be engrossed, devote himself to
4	testifying (5)	make a solemn declaration, affirm
5	speaking and not silent (9)	speak
6	teaching the word of God (11)	teach

7	persuading people (13)	entice
8	speak (14)	open his mouth

The same variety of words continues in the next verses:

- reasoned (in Ephesus, 19)

- strengthening (in Galatia, 23)

- spoke boldly, reasoning and persuading (in Ephesus, 19:8)

This helps us to understand even more about the range of possible meanings that *katangello* can carry.

Of course, if someone starts with the premise that all these Acts verbs are referring to his sermons, then they would conclude we are being told that Paul's sermons were convincing, persuasive, affirming, etc. And that person may then say, since this is how Acts describes Paul's <u>sermons</u>, this is what our sermons should be like too.

But if you don't start with that presumption, then a different picture emerges. Luke bookends this particular section of the book with his familiar concluding refrain: 'the word of God continued to increase and prevail mightily' (19:20). He is describing the advance of 'the Word', not the fortunes of 'the sermon'. Paul thought he was 'proclaiming' (1 Cor 2:1) when he was engaged in a wide range of different ways of speaking, dialoguing, convincing and converting. In fact, there are ten different verbs used of Paul's ministry in this chapter in Acts – all of which refer to speaking, but none of which can be confined to what happens in a pulpit on a Sunday during a church service.

Let's return to 1 Corinthians to consider the vocabulary that Paul himself uses to describe his task. A task that, let's remember, can be summarised as 'to know nothing among you except Jesus Christ and him crucified'.

- make firm, confirm the testimony (1:6)
- preach the gospel (1:17)
- the word of the cross (1:18)
- preaching (1:21)
- announce, proclaim (2:1)
- testimony of God (2:1)
- know (2:2)
- word (2:4)
- preaching (2:4)
- speak (2:6, 7, 13)

Paul's proclamation was far more than our familiar twenty to thirty minute sermonic monologue in a church on a Sunday morning. He did not limit his proclamation to one specific form of speaking God's Word. Paul used many different ways of speaking (without falling into the trap of aping the trickery of the verbal showmen) as he made Christ known.

The story of the gospel coming to Corinth also makes the point about the venue for preaching. It is not just in the synagogue where Paul preaches, for the gospel is equally at home next door, in the home of Titius Justus. It was there that many heard the word, believed and were baptized. Not 'in the church' but 'in the home'.

That reflects Paul's practice elsewhere too. In Acts 20, Paul describes his pattern of 'declaring', 'teaching' and 'testifying' in Ephesus, as something that he did 'in public <u>and</u> from house to house' (20). This verse does not prove that 'he never did it in a church service', of course, but it does make it crystal clear that his preaching was not restricted to the church building or church service. Everywhere he could, and at every possible opportunity, he 'did not shrink from declaring the whole counsel of God'. And the New Testament uses the preaching vocabulary to describe all of that.

We get one fascinating example of this from Paul's time in Thessalonica, a story that is told in Acts 17, during this same period of ministry. Paul explains that, whilst he was there, he did not demand the kind of financial support he was entitled to as an apostle. Instead of being a burden to any of them, he 'worked night and day' (1 Thess. 2:9), paying his own way, presumably through his tent-making occupation. But notice that Paul says in this same verse that 'we worked night and day ... while we proclaimed (*kerysso*) to you the gospel of God'. Paul was doing these two things at the same time – 'proclaiming' and 'working to earn money'. Some have even suggested that he was doing these two things <u>literally</u> at the same time: Paul 'gossiped the gospel' to his customers, over the counter, with his apron on, as he laboured and toiled for them in his leather-working workshop. No Sunday pulpit in sight! But lots and lots of preaching.

Of course, Paul is an apostle. Unique. Different from 'the ordinary Christian'! So what is <u>our</u> role in 'preaching'?

'Preaching' and Pentecostal prophesying

Let's now consider who is sent to do this preaching.

In Acts 2, Jesus, exalted to His heavenly throne, pours out His Holy Spirit on His timid, shut-away disciples so that they rush outside to speak out the gospel. The crowd can't understand how this group has become multi-lingual, so Peter explains that what is happening is what the prophet Joel had predicted. God has poured out His Spirit.

Of course the Holy Spirit had been poured out before this, in the Old Testament, on lots of occasions – on Bezalel so he could craft the tabernacle, on the elders of Numbers 11 so they could prophesy, on judges like Othniel, Gideon, Jepthah and Samson so they could rescue God's people, on kings like Saul and David so they could lead God's people, and on prophets like Ezekiel and Micah so they could speak God's Word. But through the Old Testament, the indwelling work of the Spirit was restricted to certain people to enable them to perform certain tasks at a particular moment. The surprise here is that now the Spirit is poured out 'on all flesh', that is on <u>every</u> disciple – whatever age, class or gender. There's a new one-to-one correlation: anyone who doesn't have the Spirit of Christ doesn't belong to Him (Rom. 8:9).

The Holy Spirit has been poured on me, even if I think of myself as just 'an ordinary Christian'.

And two consequences flow from this:

Every Christian knows God

The weird language about young men seeing visions, and old men dreaming dreams (in Acts 2:17f) comes from the

Old Testament. In Numbers 12:6, in a discussion about the uniqueness of God's revelation to Moses, the point is made that God does nevertheless reveal Himself to every other prophet by means of a vision or a dream. This is the normal Bible vocabulary to describe how God reveals things to prophets. So, the promise of Joel 2 is that when God pours out His Spirit on all flesh, on every believer, God will reveal Himself to every Christian, in the same way as He did to every Old Testament prophet.

And that's exactly what happens in Acts. In chapter 1, the disciples are still thoroughly confused, with little understanding of the purposes of Jesus; but in chapter 2, incredibly, they stand up and clearly preach the gospel. There's no evidence Peter had a dream or saw a vision between these two chapters. (There is a time later in Acts when he will have a vision, and it is so significant that Luke will describe it twice so we don't miss it. But that doesn't happen here.) But clearly something has changed. Peter has now received understanding through God's revelation to him.

When I became a Christian that's exactly what happened to me as well: God poured out His Spirit on me, and as He did so, He gave me an understanding of the gospel, so that I can confidently claim to know Him. Incredibly, God has opened my eyes to gospel truth. And if you are a Christian the same is true for you.

Every Christian speaks of God

Or, to use the word in Acts 2, every Christian 'prophesies'. Again in Numbers 12, we can see that receiving a dream or vision was the thing that qualified someone to speak as a prophet. If God has revealed Himself to me, then the Lord will be speaking through me as I speak out what He has said. Or, even more simply: 'the Sovereign Lord has spoken, so who can refuse to proclaim his message?' (Amos 3:8, NLT). And that's what happens in Acts 2, God pours out His Spirit, giving the disciples something to say, and for three-quarters of the chapter, Peter speaks. He is a prophet.

Peter claims that 'this is that' (16). What he is doing in Acts 2, he explains, is the prophesying of Joel 2: 'as we speak in all these tongues, we are prophesying'. And, of course, what he speaks in these different tongues is immediately understood. There's no need for interpretation because the apostles speak in the languages (and even the regional dialects) of every nation under heaven (2:5). Every language 'hears them telling in our own tongues the mighty works of God'.

What happens to Peter and the other eleven is not an experience unique to them, or to that moment in history. The quotation from Joel 2 makes it clear that when the Spirit of God is poured 'on all flesh', 'they shall prophesy'. Everyone on whom the Spirit has been poured. Every Christian.

Luke gives two very striking worked examples of this. In Acts 6:1-7, a crisis of over-work and competing priorities threatens to stunt the increase of the Word of God. The issue is resolved as a group of seven men were appointed 'to serve tables', leaving the twelve to concentrate on 'the ministry of the word and prayer'. A clear division of labour.

And so the church continues to grow. But from verse 8, Luke follows the story of Stephen, one of those seven non-Word-men, as he is taken to his trial in front of the Jewish council. Stephen then speaks out the longest speech of the book. It is true that none of the 'preaching' words are used to describe his speech, but there is little doubt that this is Word ministry! But note that it is someone who is not one of the 'professional' word ministers that does it. This is 'an ordinary Christian', a humble waiter!

A similar thing happens in chapter 8 as another of the seven table-servers, Philip, is involved in proclaiming the good news (Acts 8:4, 12) both in Samaria, and then on the desert road to Gaza. This time, two of the 'preaching' words (*euangelizomai* and *kerysso*) are used to describe what he does. There is good reason to think that Luke goes out of his way to make Philip sound like the archetypal Old Testament prophet, Elijah. But note that Luke makes this link from Elijah not to one of the twelve, 'devoted to the ministry of the word' men. No, it's the non-specialist Philip who is like the Old Testament prophet. In fact, it seems as if the story of Philip is inserted here to serve as an extended illustration of the kind of things that 'all who were scattered' were doing (8:4): this is what it looks like when regular Christian believers-who-are-prophets-but-are-not-apostles are sent out ... they preach the Word and proclaim the Christ.

Paul provides another example in Philippians. He describes the way in which his imprisonment has 'served to advance the gospel' (Phil. 1:12). The gospel has advanced firstly because Paul, now chained to a guard, has a captive audience forced to listen to him, hour after hour, day after day! The other way that the gospel has advanced is that 'most of the brothers' (presumably referring to many Christians within the Roman church) are now more boldly 'speaking the word' (14). And then Paul tells us more about this 'speaking' done by the brothers (whether it's done out of good or bad motives): when commonplace Christians 'speak' that is 'announcing' (using the *kerysso* word in 15), and 'proclaiming' (using the *katangello* word in 17 and 18). Ordinary Christians preach.

So the Day of Pentecost in Acts 2 is a moment of extraordinary democratisation! Every Christian can say; 'I have the Spirit. God has revealed to me the truth about Himself and His Son. I am now a prophet. I am to speak.' It is a hallmark of every true Christian that he knows and tells the gospel.

But there's even more to see in Acts chapter 2. Peter continues with his explanation of the quotation from Joel 2. We need to understand a bit more about Joel's prophesy to see the implication of what Peter is telling us about knowing and telling the gospel.

Joel describes a terrible locust blight that has devastated the land and people of God. There is some debate about whether Joel is describing a literal locust invasion (that was so destructive it was like the invasion of an enemy army) or a literal army invasion (that was so destructive it was like locusts). Either way, there has been 'a Day of the Locust', and this has brought the kind of destruction that God promised as judgement if His people were wayward.

National ruin like 'the Day of the Locust' should act as an early warning system for a far worse judgement that is still to come in the future, on 'the Day of the Lord'. Blood, fire and columns of smoke are things we associate with terrible suffering on this world's battlefields, or at scenes of disaster, and they are the things that will mark God's last day judgement. It will be so terrifying that the whole world will be shaking, and even the sun will bow her head in shame. 'Alas for the day ...' (that is, the past day of the locust), says Joel, because that indicates that '... the (still future) day of the Lord is near' (Joel 1:15).

We today, of course, live between these two days, after 'the Day of the Locust' and before 'the Day of the Lord'. We live in 'the last days', the final dying moments of a dying world. If the Day of Judgement is so imminent, then the obvious question is where I can go to be safe when that day comes? And the only place of safety on the Last Day is the place God provides. That's why I must call on <u>the Lord</u> now for He alone can keep me safe then. Who is this 'Lord' on whom I must call? And coming back to Acts 2, <u>that</u> is the question that the rest of Peter's sermon answers. Peter is making it clear who Joel means by 'the Lord', on whom I must call. It is 'Jesus whom you crucified', for He is the one whom God has made both Lord and Christ (Acts 2:22-36).

So Peter's sermon in Acts 2 is an extended exposition of Joel 2. What Joel prophesied is what is happening, he says. And therefore, in these Last Days, call on the one whom God has made 'the Lord' who alone can save you.

Joel says that it is in this period, in these last days, that God will pour out His Spirit. Which is exactly what God did on that Acts 2 Day of Pentecost. So now, there's nothing more on God's calendar. If the Day of the Locusts is past, and if He has poured out His Spirit (Joel 2:28-29), we know that He's about to show the wonders of verses 30-31 that will mark the end.

Let's return to the main point: God has poured out His Spirit so Christians know and tell the gospel ... and we now realise that His timescale for doing this is 'before the final Day of the Lord'.

Why? Why has God made every Christian a prophet with a message to speak? Why does God need so many mouthpieces? Why does He not continue to restrict the work of the Spirit to just the professional preacher? Or even, why not just settle for half a dozen Billy Grahams? Why does God pour His Spirit on <u>all</u> of us so <u>all</u> of us can speak?

He does this because there are millions who need to hear: <u>all</u> Christians can prophesy so that <u>all</u> can be saved. There is a link between these two 'all's. God wants a massive army of mouthpieces, millions of prophets scattered throughout the week in hospitals, schools, neighbourhoods, toddler groups, factories and labs: Christian people scattered everywhere. God sends out every Christian with an understanding of the saving work of Jesus that they are able to speak out. And He wants this to happen because there is a whole world full of people who need to hear about salvation. He longs that <u>everyone</u> knows how to be safe before the great and terrible Day of the Lord by calling on the Lord and Christ, their Saviour Jesus.

All Christians are equipped to preach good news to everyone, and we need to do so because our friends are in a desperate situation. So preach ... before 'the great and magnificent day' when God's terrible judgement will destroy everything.

Preaching in the public square

God sends all Christians into the world to preach in all kinds of ways.

There are lots of ways to 'preach'. And in line with the word-usage in the New Testament, presumably, a dialogue with my neighbour on the Number 12 bus can be described as preaching, and a defence in a courtroom can be preaching, and so can an academic paper that seeks to persuade the reader of the rational truth claims of the person of Jesus. It can happen on a street corner, or in the home. Of course, it can also happen on a Sunday morning in my local church as my church leader preaches his sermon. But it is not restricted to that one person, that one place or that one time.

God sends <u>all</u> Christians to do this, in many different ways.

Some Christians might be surprised to hear that they have been sent to do this task. Have I really been sent? Yes, we <u>are</u> sent, commissioned by the resurrection of the Lord Jesus and equipped by the Spirit that God has poured out on us. I now know the gospel and I am to tell it.

And so we are sent urgently, for the Day of the Lord is imminent. Our world needs to hear preaching. The world doesn't need us to be their Saviour, God has already provided their Saviour in the Lord Jesus, but the world does need us to be a preacher, who points them to the Lamb of God who takes away the sin of the world.

Knowing that I was writing this book, a friend recently showed me an article about Christianity being 'for the public square'. As indeed, it is. But this article interpreted 'the public square' in terms of Christian involvement in politics. I'm sure that 'the public square' includes the political arena, but it is far more than that. It is, in fact, 'the public square' ... in public, wherever people gather, wherever people meet. And into that place, all Christians are sent to be preachers.

I believe it is a mistake to shrink the categories ... so that the occasion of preaching is reduced from all Word ministry to refer to the sermon only, and so that the category of those proclaiming is reduced from every Christian to the authorised church leader only, and so that the place of proclamation is moved inside, from the world to the Christian assembly.

I believe these things because of what we have seen in the New Testament about how 'preaching' is defined and exemplified. I believe it even more strongly because of the message that we are sent to preach.

2
PREACHING THE CROSS

As we have seen in the previous chapter, we probably unconsciously import all kinds of ideas when we hear the word 'preaching'. It is no less muddy when it comes to 'the cross' bit of the phrase. And that is the topic for this chapter.

What do you have to say in a sermon for it to be accurately described as preaching 'the cross'? Does the whole sermon have to be about the cross? And which elements of 'the cross' should be included? Should the sermon describe the historical events of the crucifixion? Or are the events far less important than the meaning of those events? Must it explain the doctrine of 'penal substitution'? And if so, how extensively? What if the cross is mentioned, but only in passing – is that preaching 'the cross'? Or might it even be enough just to mention our need to be saved: would that be a preaching of 'the cross'? Or must the solution be presented as well as the problem?

What, if you like, is the irreducible minimum to include in a sermon before that can be described as 'preaching the cross'?

And, for that matter, let's extend that beyond the sermon to every Christian seeking opportunities to evangelise their friends through daily conversation: how much must be included in their 'prophesying' to make it 'preaching <u>the cross</u>'?

However we may answer that, whatever we settle upon as our irreducible minimum, that working definition must be measured alongside the New Testament. How many of the examples of sermons in the New Testament actually 'preach the cross' (by our definition)? Do the apostles actually 'preach the cross' in the book of Acts? Did Jesus ever 'preach the cross'?

Here's an opening shocker (given the title of this little book): the New Testament never uses the phrase, 'preaching the cross'!

What is preached?

Of course, the New Testament does talk about preaching the good news of peace through Jesus Christ (Acts 10:36), or preaching the unsearchable riches of Christ (Eph. 3:8), or preaching the Word (Acts 8:4) or 'the word of the cross' (1 Cor. 1:18), or Christ crucified (1 Cor. 1:23). But far and away the most common subjects for preaching are the **gospel** (e.g. Mark 1:14; Rom. 15:20; 1 Cor. 1:17; 2 Cor. 2:12, etc), or the **kingdom** (e.g. Matt. 4:17; Luke 4:43, 16:16, etc.), or both (Acts 8:12).

The Old Testament basis for this is most clearly seen in Isaiah 40 where the ideas of 'king' and 'gospel' occur together. In this chapter, three voices preach (in verses 3, 6 and 9).

The first voice speaks about getting ready. When someone famous comes, we might roll out the red carpet to make their arrival walk luxurious, and to advertise the importance of the celebrity. When God Himself comes to rescue, it's not a red carpet that's rolled out, but the whole landscape is reshaped: major earthworks fill in every valley and flatten every mountain slope to create an easy 'highway for our God' (Isa. 40:3). Here comes an extraordinarily important visitor.

The second voice explains our need: all flesh perishes. Verse 11, tells us what the coming mighty one will do about our need. We're told that the animal that most closely resembles people is sheep. Through the course _wow!_ of the Bible, we're described this way over four hundred times. Sheep aren't clever. Sheep are helpless when they fall onto their backs. Sheep stumble off cliffs. Sheep eat the wrong things. Sheep run off. Sheep get lost. Sheep are completely feeble and desperately need a shepherd. All people are 'sheep-ish'! And that's a way of saying that we need help. We might like to imagine that we're invincible, but of course we're not: we 'wither' (6-8).

The third voice is like the sergeant-at-arms who announces that royalty has arrived. In the days before microphones and a PA system, you had to go up onto a high mountain and 'lift up your voice with strength' if you wanted to be heard. That's where this announcer goes to bellow out the news: 'Behold your God' (9). Cue trumpet fanfare. Here He is!

And as this God comes, it's as if He's rolling up His sleeve: can you see His mighty, strong arm (10)? The powerful God Himself is coming to do the huge task that verse 11 describes: I'm coming to rescue you – to tend and gather and carry and lead you.

The **gospel** is that **the King** is coming.

And when the Lord Jesus Christ came, John the Baptist shone the spotlight onto Him, quoting words from Isaiah 40:3 to say: 'Look: here he is.' Jesus has come to be who Isaiah 40 pointed to, and to do what Isaiah 40 described. So as Jesus Himself preached the **gospel**, He announced the **kingdom** (Mark 1:14-15).

In his book *Know and Tell the Gospel*, the late Australian evangelist John Chapman debates the relationship between 'the gospel' and 'the kingdom of God'. He notes that sometimes people have divided these two ideas – for example by suggesting that Jesus preached the kingdom, whereas Paul preached the gospel. But, as he clearly shows, this is to invent a false dichotomy: Jesus is both Saviour and Lord. 'Jesus is able to save us from sin and death because He has overthrown and defeated Satan. He is able to save because He is Lord. It is not possible to accept Jesus as Saviour and not as Lord since He has saved us by being Lord.'[1]

In short, the **gospel** of the New Testament is a declaration about the **kingdom** – the reign of King Jesus. The appropriate response to such a gospel and to such a king is, of course, 'the obedience of faith' – 'to turn to God in repentance and have faith in our Lord Jesus' (Acts 20:21).

I have just been listening to an astonishing Christmas sermon on Revelation 12. The speaker noted that Matthew tells the Christmas story in terms of wise men searching

---

1   John Chapman: *Know and Tell the Gospel* (St Matthias, 1998) p. 35.

for the king. Luke tells the Christmas story of shepherds summoned by the angels. And the Apostle John tells the Christmas story of a Dragon in the Maternity Hospital! This is an extraordinarily graphic image, of a beast looking for babies to devour, but it sets up the proclamation of the same gospel: the Lamb defeats the Dragon, His blood silences Satan's accusations, and the Son's reign throws the devil down.

That is a public truth that's worth preaching!

Let's lean forward to listen more attentively to this preaching in the New Testament.

What is preached in the gospels

Over the last few years, I have come to a mind-shifting realisation. I'd thought that the word 'gospel' in Mark 1:1 referred to the literary form of the book. We have four gospels, written by four people who gave us the four books: Matthew's Gospel, Mark's Gospel, etc. But of course it wasn't until the second century that the word 'gospel' began to be used that way.

When Mark tells us that he is writing 'the beginning of the gospel of Jesus Christ, the Son of God', he is using the word 'gospel' in the same way that it is used elsewhere in the Bible. Mark knew this gospel well for he had heard lots of apostolic preaching as a fellow-worker of Paul and Barnabas on their missionary journeys. And what he writes is a book of that gospel preaching, heard and learnt from the apostles, and written down for us.

Mark 1:1 introduces the theme of his book: the gospel. The wording of this verse bears a striking resemblance to a calendar inscription from about 9 B.C. that has been found in Priene in Asia Minor. Speaking about the Emperor Octavian Augustus (referred to as 'the god'), 'the birthday of the god was for the world *the beginning of the gospel* which has been proclaimed on his account'. William Lane suggests that this inscription sets Mark's preface within the cult of the emperor, and clarifies for us 'the essential content of an *evangel* in the ancient world: an historical event, which introduces a new situation for the world'[2].

That is, of course, what Jesus says: 'The time is fulfilled, and the kingdom of God is at hand; repent and believe in the gospel' (Mark 1:14-15). Notice that three ideas are brought together:

- a new, decisive moment in history
- the 'at hand-ness' of the kingdom of God
- repenting-and-believing as the appropriate response.

At this historic moment, something cataclysmic is happening, for God's King has come into this world to save people from this world for the next. This will upturn the whole of your life!

Mark 1:1 then gives two titles for Jesus that will be used to structure Mark's gospel proclamation into two halves. At 8:29, at the half-way point, Peter declares 'You are the Christ', and at 15:39, at the cross, a centurion declares 'this man was the Son of God'. These two statements divide the story into two halves: the first half is concerned with who Jesus the Christ truly is, and the second with what that Son

2   William Lane, *The Gospel of Mark* (NICNT, Eerdmans, 1974) pp. 42-43.

of God[3] came to do. And it is not until Peter has learnt lesson one, who the Christ is, that Jesus can begin to teach him lesson two, that He came to die (cf 'began to teach' in 8:31). For it is a most extraordinary thing that, rather than coming to earth to lord it over us, this king came to be our servant by giving His life as a ransom for many (Mark 10:32-45). The King ... and the Cross. The Lord ... who saves (which is what the name 'Jesus' means of course).

Can you see how close this is to the verse we've kept returning to in 1 Corinthians 2:2? The summary of the gospel Paul preached is 'Jesus Christ and him crucified'. That would work as a good title for Mark's gospel; 'Jesus the Christ (= Part One) ... and him crucified (= Part Two)'.

It also matches the argument of Acts 2:22-23. In Peter's Pentecost sermon, as he proclaims that 'the Lord' is Jesus, verse 22 summarises the first half of Mark's gospel – the mighty works and wonders and signs that God did through Jesus to attest Him. Verse 23 describes the cross to which He must go, 'according to the definite plan and foreknowledge of God'. Here is the gospel. It's all about Jesus: (a) what He did; and (b) what was done to Him.

These two themes are inextricably linked. In his commentary, Hugh Anderson makes the point that 'only in and through his death on the cross can it be known who Jesus truly is, the one in whom God seeks out men

3   'Son of God' is not really a doctrinal declaration that Jesus is 'God the Son', the second person of the Trinity. Rather, it is almost synonymous with the title, 'the Christ' (cf Luke 22:67-70), whose antecedents are Adam, Israel and David (cf Graeme Goldsworthy, *The Son of God and the New Creation* [Crossway, 2015]).

to save them'.[4] That is Mark's gospel: if you can see what the centurion saw, standing and looking at 'the obscurity, lowliness and humiliation of the cross', and then say what the centurion said, you have understood the gospel. It is not enough to declare Him as the Christ; we must also understand what kind of Christ He is.

Many prefer the misunderstanding. James and John become the spokespeople for all of us who like the idea of Jesus as King, so long as we can have positions alongside Him when He is 'in his glory' (10:37), acclaimed as world emperor in a moment of magnificent triumph. But of course, in asking for this, they clearly 'do not know what (they) are asking'. Jesus' moment of glory is the cross, for that is where people are rescued, Satan is defeated and death is destroyed: the rejected stone made into the marvellous cornerstone (12:10-11). James and John aren't thinking that 'glory' equals 'death'. They don't realise that, in effect, they are asking to be the two robbers hung on crosses either side of Jesus' glorious cross. 'Do you really want that?!' is Jesus' question. This ignominious, shameful, despised execution is what it means to follow Jesus, to deny yourself in this world, for the sake of being great in the world to come.

This is why, of course, 'repentance' is the message – of Jesus (Mark 1:14-15), and also of His forerunner (1:4) and, later, of the apostles Jesus would send (6:12). To follow Jesus means a complete turn-around of all my priorities: to turn away from idols to serve the living God

4   Hugh Anderson, *The Gospel of Mark* (New Century, Oliphants, 1976) p. 348.

(Acts 14:15; 1 Thess. 1:9-10); to turn from the perspective of Satan and instead to 'set our minds on things of God'; to lose my life in this world for the sake of the world to come. By the cross of the Lord Jesus Christ, 'the world has been crucified to me, and I to the world' (Gal. 6:14). The cost of following this Son of Man is great. It's treating every pleasure in this world, every achievement, every conquest, everything that we would consider marks us out ... to 'count them as rubbish' (Phil. 3:8) because life in the next world is incomparably more important than life in this world.

To be clear: this message of this cataclysmic event is not going to be welcomed. And Mark 6:1-29 makes it clear what fate should be expected for all preachers saying such things: John is silenced, Jesus will be crucified, and His disciples should prepare for those who 'will not listen to you'. But this is the gospel that Mark preaches.

What is preached in Acts

Chris Green has analysed the apostolic sermons in the book of Acts.[5] He notes that Luke initially tells us a full outline of what Peter or Paul or whoever 'typically' preached, and then, as the book goes on, provides summaries that become more and more concise. Luke rarely repeats himself. For example, the first full-blown evangelistic sermon is twenty-two verses (2:14-36), the next is fourteen verses (3:12-26), the third is just five (4:8-11, 19-20), and the fourth summarises it into a highly concentrated three verses (5:29-32).

---

5   Chris Green, *The Word of his Grace* (IVP, 2005) pp. 26-30.

This means that the basic content of the apostles' preaching is very clear. The condensed version is:

- *you* killed Him;
- *God* raised Him;
- *we* saw Him.

For those who had not been present at the crucifixion (for example, in 10:36-41), who had therefore not had personal experience of Jesus' ministry, nor been responsible for His death, that basic version is supplemented with some introductory information about who Jesus was, and then the three points are adapted to:

- *they* (not *you*) killed Him;
- *God* raised Him;
- *we* saw Him.

And then still later in Acts, when Paul preaches the gospel to a mixed audience of both Jews and Gentiles (for example, in 13:16-42), even further removed from the events, the outline is adapted still further. The introduction is enlarged to provide an Old Testament background about the Messiah, followed by information about who Jesus was. And then the three points follow:

- *they* (not *you*) killed Him;
- *God* raised Him;
- *they* (not *we*) saw Him.

The importance of this is that there is a clear and consistent content to the gospel that the apostles preached.

Additional elements may need adding according to the particular audience, but the basic structure remains the same.

The first of these three elements in 'the Acts gospel' concerns the death of Jesus, and in particular, the personal culpability for that death. Wicked people are held responsible that the Holy and Righteous One was 'denied' and the Author of life 'killed' (3:13-14). The High Priest is right to think that 'you intend to bring this man's blood on us', for Peter charges that yes indeed, 'you killed [him] by hanging him on a tree' (5:30). 'You have betrayed and murdered' the Righteous One (7:52).

The second concerns the resurrection of Jesus, who was raised not just to life (2:30-32) but also to reign (2:33): 'exalted at his right hand as Leader and Saviour' (5:31). A day has now been fixed on which God 'will judge the world in righteousness by a man whom he has appointed; and of this he has given assurance to all by raising him from the dead' (17:30-31). And on that day, sinners will 'be astounded and perish' (13:41).

Therefore, because we are guilty sinners and our judge is coming, we need salvation. 'And there is salvation in no one else, for there is no other name under heaven given among men by which we must be saved' (4:12). That is how 'we believe that we will be saved through the grace of the Lord Jesus' (15:11).

To note the third point in our gospel summaries, Luke's précis of the apostles' preaching in 4:33 is instructive: they 'were giving their testimony to the resurrection of the Lord Jesus'. That is it! Certainly, that is the topic that greatly annoyed the temple authorities: 'they were teaching the people and proclaiming in Jesus the resurrection from the dead' (4:1-3). It is similarly the implications of this same theme that caused opposition from the city authorities in Thessalonica: 'they are all acting against the decrees of Caesar, saying that there is another king, Jesus' (17:3, 6-7). The **gospel** is about the **king**.

Conclusion

Let us draw together the themes of this New Testament gospel.

It concerns Jesus, born in the city of David, to be our Saviour (Luke 2:11). Romans 1:1-5 confirms that because this Jesus is in David's family line, He is therefore qualified to be the king, and since He was raised from the dead, He is thereby qualified-and-declared to be The King, who will rule over all the nations of God's world for ever (Ps. 2:8).

He is indeed the Christ (Acts 8:5), the awesome, all-authoritative King of all. He is The Son of God that Adam, Israel, David and all their descendants failed to be (Luke 3:22, in the light of Jesus' perfect obedience in the wilderness in 4:1-13). He brings in the year of liberty and the year of the Lord's favour (Luke 4:18-19 quoting Isaiah 61 to make it plain that His ministry is all about the reign of God and His return to Zion). His healing miracles are signs that Jesus is the Lord who has come to bring salvation to Zion (see Isa. 35).

Jesus is raised to life (1 Cor. 15:12) as the firstborn from the dead (Col. 1:18), He has been appointed by God to be the Judge of all the living and the dead (Acts 10:42).

We might be asking how the cross fits into this gospel. This book is entitled 'Preaching the Cross'!

This glorious King Jesus is the one who was scandalously crucified. 'Here is the Son' that the tenants killed in order to steal His inheritance (Mark 12:7). 'My shepherd', smitten by God Himself, but for our iniquities (Isa. 53:4-6). A stone that the builders rejected (1 Pet. 1:7) is now a marvellous thing, for it is 'the power of God' to us who are being saved (1 Cor. 1:17). For when His priceless blood (1 Pet. 1:18) was shed, He ransomed people for God from every ethnic group (Rev. 5:9-10) and for ever (Heb. 10:14): 'the dignity of an infinite person swallows up ... all the infinities of punishment due to us'[6]. His appearance – the goodness and loving kindness of God our Saviour - saved us (Titus 2:11; 3:4).

To summarise: the <u>news</u> is that the King has come. And what turns that news into <u>good</u> news is that this King died for my sin.

This is no new gospel, but what was 'promised beforehand through his prophets in the holy Scriptures' (Rom. 1:2). We should find it referenced in the whole Bible. The whole Bible is about it. It is the melody that every part of the Bible sings.

This is a gospel with huge dimensions! Having seen the depth, breadth and implications of the gospel that was proclaimed, we should be wary of a reductionist mentality that shrinks the content we preach when we are 'preaching the cross'.

---

6   Turretin, *Institutes* vol 2, 14.XI.xxx, p. 437.

3
WHY WORDS?

In these first three chapters, we're trying to define some issues that lie behind the topic of this book, before the main thesis which will come in the next chapter. Hang in there!

In Chapter 1, we saw that 'preaching' is not the same as 'giving sermons'. There are many ways to 'preach'. And every Christian, through the gift of the Holy Spirit, has had revelation given to them so that they now proclaim or prophesy or preach.

In Chapter 2, we thought more about what it is that Christians proclaim. Of course, we proclaim Jesus. But this 'gospel' is a much larger category than we may imagine. It centres on God the Lord of kings, who has given to Jesus 'dominion and glory and a kingdom that all peoples, nations and languages should serve him; his dominion is an everlasting kingdom, which shall not pass away, and his kingdom one that shall not be destroyed' (Dan. 7:14). The content of the New Testament gospel is that this risen Jesus Christ is Lord, that there is forgiveness in His name, and that this is something to be heralded to all the world.

Here is the third question.

What is the link between these first two chapters – the gospel, and the preaching of the gospel? Why does it matter that this Jesus is 'preached'? Why is it that speaking it is so important?

We need to take some steps back and ask how God works in His world.

A short Biblical theology of 'the word'

Andrew Wilson has written a brilliant retelling of the Bible story-as-a-single-story.

It starts like this:

> In the beginning, God. Everything was shapeless, and empty, and dark. Blobs of unsorted, unformed matter drifting through space. An enormous cosmic splodge. A scribble.

> And God said, 'Lights.' And it happened.

> And God said, and it happened. And God said, and it happened. And God said, and the earth did. And God said, and the animals did.

> And God said ...[1]

The power of the Word of God is extraordinary. God spoke, and things would just ... be. 'God's revelation begins with a sermon; God preaches and the world is made. God said "Let there be light", and there was light. Six sermons are preached in a wonderful sequence; the Word of God is proclaimed in heaven's pulpit and all comes to pass. The preaching forms the universe'.[2]

---

1   Andrew Wilson, *Unbreakable* (10 Publishing, 2014) pp. 11-12.
2   Quoted in Peter Adam, *Speaking God's Words* (IVP, 1996) p. 15.

'By the Word of the Lord the heavens were made, and by the breath of his mouth all their host' (Ps. 33:6). Everything was 'formed out of water and through water by the word of God' (2 Pet. 3:5). As he brings the world into being, 'God's point of contact with the world is his word'[3].

And now, the powerful Word of Jesus upholds everything that has been made (Heb. 1:3) in Him, through Him and for Him (Col. 1:15-20).

So, of course, Satan the serpent focuses his attack on this Word of God. Knock that domino down and watch the effect throughout creation. He questions the *clarity* of what God says, because 'we can't really be sure, can we? deciphering what he means is so difficult!' He questions the *truthfulness* of God's words: 'I thought you believed in a God of love, so surely He won't send people to hell!' He questions the *goodness* of God's Word by suggesting that 'he seems so restrictive and ungenerous, determined to spoil your fun' (Gen. 3:1-5).

And it is this same Word that the Planning Department of Babel City rejects. But they 'plot in vain' (Ps. 2:1). When people defy His word by gathering together to build a city (Gen. 11:4 cf 9:1, 7), the Lord disperses them anyway (Gen. 11:9). When they want universal brand recognition to impress everyone (Gen. 11:4), the Lord overlooks their barely-visible pile of Lego building blocks and instead makes great the name of the person He chooses (Gen. 12:2).

---

3   John Woodhouse, *God of Word* (Matthias Media, 2015) p. 11.

What will God do when people reject His Word? Against the backdrop of such defiance, God makes promises. He speaks more words! God announced 'the gospel in advance' to Abraham (Gal. 3:8): this is 'the text the rest of the Bible expounds'[4] for God's Word determines everything that will happen.

By the time the book of Exodus opens, the family tree element of the Genesis 12 promise is well on the way to being fulfilled – from one old man to twelve sons (Exod. 1:2-4), to an extended family of seventy (1:5), to a 'landfill' of a family (if that's the right collective noun!) (1:7), to maybe two million-plus (by 12:37). Note then that Pharaoh's attempted genocide (1:8-22) is a challenge to God's spoken promise. Which will triumph – a world superpower, or a word from God?

Of course, it is what God says. And through the Exodus, He ties His character to His Word: He wants to be always known as 'the Lord', the One who says He will redeem (Exod. 6:1-8), and then does so whilst His people sit down, shut up and watch (Exod. 14:13-14)! What God says, always wins.

At Sinai, the Exodus generation 'gathers to hear' (Deut. 4:9-14), for the way that this Old Testament 'church' (Acts 7:38) relates to God is always-and-only by a word. But the people rebel against this powerful word of promise that they have enjoyed (Ps. 107:11), so need to learn that they can only experience life 'by every word that comes from his mouth' (Exod. 8:3). The 'Promised' Land is exactly that: a place of life provided by God's words of promise.

4   Vaughan Roberts, *God's Big Picture* (IVP, 2002) p. 53.

Finally arriving in the land of prosperity from the land of austerity, the big take-home lesson for the people of Israel is that everything happened because of 'the word that the Lord swore to Abraham, to Isaac, and to Jacob' (Deut. 9:5). With Martin Luther, we might say 'the Word did it all.' 'Not one word has failed of all the good things that the Lord your God promised concerning you. All have come to pass for you; not one of them has failed' (Josh. 23:14). And it is not long before conquest of the whole of the land of promise is achieved, establishing 'the border of Israel from Lebo-hamath as far as the Sea of the Arabah, according to the word of the Lord, the God of Israel' (2 Kings 14:25). God said. That's why it happened.

After a king is provided, 2 Samuel 7 is full of remarkable words of God promising to establish 'the throne of his kingdom forever' (7:13). David, the king that God chose to set His heart on,[5] knows to pray that God will 'confirm forever the word that you have spoken ... and do as you have spoken' (7:25). Kings may come and go, 'the grass withers, the flower fades, but the word of our God will stand forever' (Isa. 40:8).

Of course, every ruling king of Israel needs to learn that his rule is under the rule of God, and that means living under God's Word. Every king is therefore anointed by the prophet and accountable to the prophet, and every king is assessed by the criterion of obedience to the word the prophet has spoken. 'Has the Lord as great delight

---

5   This is what 1 Samuel 13:14 means, according to John Woodhouse in *The Proclamation Bible*, Introduction to 1 and 2 Samuel (Hodder & Stoughton, 2013).

in burnt offerings and sacrifices as in obeying the voice of the Lord? Behold, to obey is better than sacrifice' (1 Sam. 15:22). That's God's message to the hard-of-hearing Saul: you are not above the Word of God.

And what is true for the king is true for the people: God has spoken; will you listen? 'If you faithfully obey the voice of the Lord your God …' there will be great blessing; but 'if you will not obey the voice of the Lord your God …' then 'the Lord will send on you curses, confusion and frustration in all that you undertake to do' (Deut. 28:1-20). In either eventuality, what God has spoken is what will determine all that happens to you (even, ironically, whilst you are engaged in trying to ignore the very thing that God has spoken)!

God warned: 'cursed be the man who does not hear the words of this covenant' (Jer. 11:3). Israel 'would not listen' (2 Kings 17:14), so 'behold, I am bringing upon this city and upon all its towns all the disaster that I have pronounced against it, because they have stiffened their neck, refusing to hear my words' (Jer. 19:15). God 'pronounced' and so things come to be. And amongst all the terrible curses that will fall, one of the most frightening is the news that God promises days ahead 'when I will send a famine on the land – not a famine of bread, nor a thirst for water, but of hearing the words of the Lord' (Amos 8:11). The punishment for rejecting God's Word is to live without God's Word. Exile from the land of promise is inevitable.

What could change the inevitability of this horrifying outcome? Only God's Word! He speaks again. Prophets are sent armed with nothing but words from above: 'Your words were found, and I ate them, and your words became to me a joy and the delight of my heart' (Jer. 15:16). Even an amateur prophet, more comfortable amongst his figs, tells how 'the Lord God said to me, "Go prophesy to my people Israel". Now therefore hear ...' (Amos 7:14-15). What could I do but tell you what God says?

And what does God say? He promises a second Exodus. Another redemption. From judgement and death to salvation and life. All of it is to be achieved because God purposes it, and speaks it into being: 'I will, I will, I will!' '[My word will not] return to me empty, but it shall accomplish that which I purpose' (Isa. 55:10-11).

When the Redeemer comes to bring the promised redemption, He comes as a man of words, preaching (Mark 1:38), calling (Mark 2:17) and gathering a new people around Him and His words (Luke 8:21) 'for he whom God has sent utters the words of God' (John 3:34). Where else could people go, for it is Jesus who has 'the words of eternal life' (John 6:68)? Crowds press in on Him to hear not simply what He says, but 'the word of God' that they recognise (Luke 5:1). He sows the powerful seed of the Word of God (Mark 4:1-34) that is certain to produce a harvest. Of course it will. How could the Word of God fail to achieve its objective? So there will be a harvest of people 'born again, not of perishable seed, but of imperishable, through the living and abiding word of God' (1 Pet. 1:23).

This Word has such power that, of course, Jesus sends out His followers to 'preach the word' (Mark 3:14). And every subsequent church leader commits himself 'to the public reading of Scripture, to exhortation, to preaching' (1 Tim. 4:13), that is, to this same task: 'to speak the word of God' (Heb. 13:7), as a workman 'rightly handling the word of truth' (2 Tim. 2:15). For that is Christian ministry, according to the stewardship that is from God: 'to make the word of God fully known' (Col. 1:25). The spread of Christianity is actually the story of the spread of this Word of God (Acts 6:7; 12:24; 19:20), for it is the Word being spoken that advances the gospel (Phil. 1:12-18). No wonder that Acts ends with that continuing task of still more 'proclaiming' and 'teaching' (Acts 28:30-31).

One of the New Testament's most common descriptions of Christians is 'those who are called', for that is how baby Christians are born – 'by the word of truth' (James 1:18), 'through the living and abiding word of God ... the good news that was preached to you' (1 Pet. 1:22, 24). They 'accepted (what you heard from us) not as the word of men but as what it actually is, the word of God, which is at work in you believers' (1 Thess. 2:13). So the sheep that Jesus knows are those who listen to his voice (John 10:16).

No wonder the whole Bible ends with the instruction to 'keep the words of this book' (Rev. 22:9), neither adding to them (22:18) nor subtracting from them (22:19). Of course. For the Word of God that interrupted the silence at the start of everything will similarly interrupt the noisy bustle of everything to bring it to an end. And then will come the time 'when all who are in the tombs will hear his voice and come out, those who have done good to the resurrection of life, and those who have done evil to the resurrection of judgement' (John 5:28-29). What delight we will have to hear our Lord and Master speak to us, one more time: 'Well done good and faithful servant. Enter into the joy of your Master' (Matt. 25:21-22).

God speaks. And His words are tied to his actions. 'In Biblical language and theology, God speaking and God acting are often one and the same thing.'[6] His powerful voice is like the roar of a lion (Amos 3:8), or like the roar of many waters, or like a sharp two-edged sword (Rev. 1:15-16).

Wow!

A word to preach

This mini Bible overview should make one thing very clear to us: if God wants something to happen, He just has to speak it into being. His Word is powerful.

One of the most graphic Bible stories to make this point is set in the valley of lost hope in Ezekiel 37.

The situation is that Israel are guilty of sin and God has poured out His wrath on them (Ezek. 36:17-18). Israel has divided. The Northern Kingdom has been swallowed up by Assyria and basically disappears from history. The people of the Southern Kingdom have been scattered to Babylon, where, ten years later, they hear that their beloved Jerusalem is destroyed – both the 'house' of their forever king David, and the 'House' of God where the King of Kings dwelt. No wonder God's people sat down and

6   Timothy Ward, *Words of Life* (IVP, 2009) p. 28.

wept, whilst their captors mock them by insisting they sing one of their happy-clappy worship songs (Ps. 137:1-4). But here in exile, with God against them, they couldn't sing anything. They are just like a valley of dry bones.

We're used to seeing modern images of mass death on TV news – unearthed graves, piles of skulls and skeletons, severed limbs after street explosions and bloated corpses after tsunamis. But none of these quite matches the horror of the sickening vision of this vast valley covered in unburied human bones. Ezekiel had actually been in this valley previously at the start of his ministry when 'the glory of the Lord stood there' (3:23). But now the valley is grim, rather than glorious. Fragmentary remains of people no longer identifiable, stripped bare by vultures, and scorched white by the sun. No hint of life wherever he looked. Of course if you're a dog, this is heaven! But for Ezekiel, a Jew, to remain unburied is a mark of God's curse. And even worse for Ezekiel, who as a trainee priest would never be allowed to touch a human corpse, he is led right through the middle of it all.

Extraordinarily, into a valley of lost hope like this, God speaks, promising to cleanse (36:25) and to change (36:26-37). There has to be a total reboot – a rebirth by water and the Spirit, as Jesus will say to Nicodemus, using the imagery of this vision (in John 3:5). God promises life. But how will God bring life to such an extreme landscape of death? What is Ezekiel supposed to reply when God asks if these bones can live? It's a QI moment! He gives the best answer: 'O Lord God, you know'. For, obviously if these bones are to live, God, who has promised (in chapter 36) that 'I will ... I will ... I will ...', must do it. Who else could?

Ezekiel 37:4 is therefore an extraordinary moment in the story. Yes, these bones can live, should the Sovereign Lord choose to bring them to life. Yes, they can live, should the Creator God put His life-giving breath into them. Yes, there can be a future in such a valley of dry bones, but only if ... what? Someone preaches the Word of God!

Can you imagine what it felt like to be Ezekiel, on his own in a valley like this, standing in the middle of thousands and thousands of bones and telling them to get up!

And isn't this _exactly_ how it feels for any one of us to speak out the Word of God? It may be that we are speaking to unbelieving friends and it seems so foolish to talk about the death of Jesus to them. It may be that we are leading the youth group epilogue: can my talk really interest these reluctant teenagers, let alone affect them? Or for those of us who preach sermons, we look out at what seems like rows and rows of 'dead bones' in our Sunday congregations (!) and wonder if there is any point speaking the message I've prepared. Is it really the case that speaking the Word of God could make a difference? It's painfully obvious that _we_ can't bring life to people who are dead in their trespasses and sins. We could never get a lifeless, stone heart to warm to truth. But the Sovereign Creator God can. And He chooses to do it through His Word.

Ezekiel proclaimed the Word of God and bones came together. He spoke to the wind, and like breath breathed

into the man of dust in Genesis 2, living creatures are able
to stand on their feet – an exceedingly great army.

Well ...!

You doubt the power of the Word of God? How was
it then that you were brought from death to life? Was it
not that someone spoke to you? In my case, it was my
mum and dad, and some Sunday School teachers, and
youth group leaders, and student friends and preachers.
At various times, over many years, they spoke truth to me,
and the Word they spoke transformed me. Powerful, isn't
it, this Word of God? And of course what is true for me
is similarly true for every Christian in my church. There
are many different stories of the path we all followed to
be in the same church together now, but all our stories
will feature Christians who spoke the Word of God to us:
this Word is very powerful, isn't it? And of course what is
true for all those I know is just as true for every Christian
the world over: it was the proclamation of the gospel that
was powerful enough to save them. And what is true of
all Christians alive today is true for every Christian that
there has ever been: the Word was the means God used
to deliver us all from the domain of darkness and transfer
us to the kingdom of light. Through the proclamation of
Jesus, God made alive all of us who were dead in our
trespasses and sins (Col. 1:24-2:15).

Ezekiel 37 tells us that a world under the judgement of
God has no greater need than to hear the Word of God.
Dead people need God's Word because, without it, they
stay dead. And Ezekiel 37 tells us that proclaiming that
Word of God is the most powerful thing that you and I can

do: God sends a proclaimer because that is the means
God uses to regenerate.

So, where is the power of God?

It is the gospel that 'is the power of God for salvation to
everyone who believes' (Rom. 1:16). It is 'the word of the
cross' that, for us who are being saved, 'is the power of
God' (1 Cor. 1:18). It is by 'the word of truth' that God
brought us forth (James 1:18). It is 'through the living and
abiding word of God' that we have been born again
(1 Pet. 1:23). And on and on.

The word does so much

I remember very clearly the time in our lives when my
wife and I were convinced of all this. I was already a church
worker, but my ministry lacked sharpness: to be honest,
I don't think I really knew what I was doing! For my wife
it was Romans 1:16-17 that brought home to her that the
gospel is powerful: we just need to speak it. For me it was
Colossians 1:28-29. Proclaiming Jesus is what I needed
to do if I wanted to present people mature in Christ on
the Last Day. We grew in these convictions. It took huge
pressure off us, and gave enormous clarity about our task
as Christians, and the shape of our future life together. Our
job was simply to speak out God's Word.

In 2 Timothy 3:14–4:5, 'the Word' is given a whole
range of roughly equivalent names in the surrounding
verses: the sacred writings (3:15), Scripture (3:16), sound
(or healthy) teaching (4:3) or the truth (4:4). Paul's single
point is that this Word is what is 'able to make you wise
for salvation' and this same Word is to be used 'for
teaching, for reproof, for correction, and for training

in righteousness'. This 'Word' is able to make people Christian and to keep people Christian; it has within it – or even more accurately, that it is, in and of itself – everything that is required to evangelise and to disciple. So a church minister (like Timothy) with the Bible in his hand has got everything that he needs to do the job: he is fully equipped (17). And since God has given the church minister the complete toolbox for ministry, his job now is simply to put that Word to work (4:2).

Why words? Well simple: it is because God's Words work.

The power of God is not in the pulpit. Or, at least, it is only in the pulpit in so far as the Word of God is in the pulpit. It is not in the preacher. Or, at least, it is only in the preacher in so far as the things that he says are the Word of God. It is not in the sermon. Or, at least, it is only in the sermon if it is preaching the Bible truly.

The place of proclamation, the person doing the proclaiming, the literary shape of the proclamation are not the determinative factors.

The power of God is in the Word of God.

Preach the Word!

4
LITTLE AND LARGE

And so, now, we turn to the thesis of this book. 'At last', I hear you say!

Imagine that you have just come back from a wonderful summer holiday. You've been refreshed through reading great classics and had time to clear the mind, to think, plan and pray. 'Right,' you determine, 'my life is going to change. I'm going to read a couple of chapters from a book every morning from now on.'

This week's book is *Pride and Prejudice*, and today you're reading Chapter 12. The third and fourth paragraphs particularly interest you. You see that the subject is 'the master of the house'. And you note that, several lines later, someone else gives advice to Elizabeth, the heroine, 'to be particularly careful'. Aha, you say, this is like a message from God Himself for me today ... He is like my 'master', and He is telling me to 'be careful'.

It's an absurd example, of course.

But, it's not so far away from how lots of Christians approach reading the Bible in personal morning devotions. Some phrase or other seems important to us ... we note what it says ... make a connection from the words we've read to us in our situation ... and this becomes 'the Lord's Word for me today'.

But every bit of the Bible is not written about us. It is <u>for</u> us. But it is not <u>about</u> us.

Each word we read comes as part of a sentence. Each sentence comes as part of a paragraph. Paragraphs build together to create chapters. And a collection of chapters makes a book. And the books of the Bible are volumed together to create our Bibles.

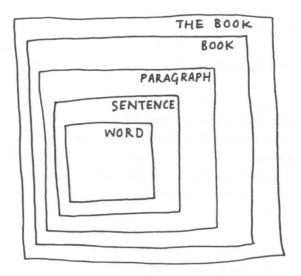

We are used to hearing that if you take a text out of its context, you are left with a con! But now we're extending the point beyond the paragraphs that immediately surround a particular verse to include the widest possible context of 'all that the Bible says'. There is a direct connection between any individual element that we find in the Bible and the big overall salvation plan of God (which is the subject of the Bible from first page to last).

The 'little' must be kept firmly embedded in the 'large'.

This connection between 'little' and 'large' is the theme of this chapter. Whenever we're preaching the cross (where those terms are defined in the way we've been exploring), the 'little' and the 'large' go together. One 'little' single phrase in the Bible needs to be set firmly in the 'large' context of its sentence, paragraph, chapter, book and Biblical theology. At the same time, the 'large', many centuries-long, single-storyline of the Bible is always pointing to the last 'little' piece that completes the picture: Jesus at the heart of it all.

Let's explore those ideas.

The little implies the large

At the Cornhill Training Course, we currently listen to over 1,300 students' practice sermons per year, each given in the context of a small group workshop. Obviously, I don't listen to them all (!), and we are hugely grateful to many church ministers who help us in the important task of offering valuable feedback and advice. I do try to read a lot of the written comments that are sent to the students after each of their talks. As you might imagine, some common themes and mistakes are quickly apparent.

One of the most common critiques is what we call the 'bouncing ball' syndrome: 'this verse reminds me of some other Bible passage/some other theological theme; let me "bounce off" this passage and tell you about that instead.'

There are many reasons why a young preacher might be fond of bouncing the ball! One reason is a lack of sharpness in observing what the text <u>actually</u> says, so the preacher just observes the general topic and bounces off that to tell us many other things about the same subject, without telling us <u>exactly</u> what this passage wants to say to us about it <u>here</u>. One example, from a talk just this past week, was when a passage talked about Christ's work of 'reconciling' us in his body of flesh by his death (Col. 1:22). The speaker talked about Christ's redeeming work, paying the price for our salvation. Do you see what has happened there? The passage describes the achievement of the cross in terms of 'reconciliation', and the speaker talked not about that but about two other images – 'redemption' and 'salvation'.

Often, the young preacher bounces the ball like that because his theological framework suggests that there's more to be said than this passage says. So I use my passage as the hyperlink to a search engine on that topic. For example, if I am talking about 'the cross', then there is a broad list of ideas that the Bible uses, and I must include all those ideas. I must be exhaustive to be accurate. Yes, the cross achieves reconciliation, <u>and</u> redemption, <u>and</u> salvation, <u>and</u> ... ! On some topics, my theological framework may be extensive, so I recognise that I can't possibly say <u>everything</u> I know. But if I can't be exhaustive, my framework tells me that there are certain elements that I must not omit. For example, in any talk of the cross, I must bounce off whatever my passage says to include the fact that 'Jesus was punished in my place'.

In other words, I am considering the 'little', and feel that I need to bounce off that to talk about the 'large'.

But let's press pause for a moment. What is the gospel that we are to proclaim[1]? Why is 'Jesus was punished in my place' the irreducible minimum? What about 'God has made Jesus both Lord and Christ': doesn't that have to be included too? Or that I am storing up wrath for myself on the day of wrath because of my sins. Or that God has fixed a day on which He will judge the world by Jesus, whom He has appointed. Or that God reconciles His enemies. And so on. It's difficult to justify omitting those elements too, isn't it?

Here's an alternative proposal: the gospel is not so much a checklist as a worldview. It is the worldview that the Bible gives to us. And every time I talk about any single element in the Bible, or in that worldview, anything I say will relate to the overall bigger picture. The 'little' will imply the 'large'.

Here's an image to explain this proposal[2]. Imagine that the story of the whole of God's redemptive plan is a huge pie, baked in a massive circular pie dish. And imagine cutting a single slice from that pie. That little portion – even if it is the tiniest sliver – implies the shape of the entire pie. The angles, the curved outer edge, the length of each side ... all of those elements make it clear that this wedge is a part of a bigger whole. It comes from a large circular pie.

---

1   See Chapter 2.
2   I first learnt this image from Phillip Jensen but I may have adapted it so completely that it's no longer what he originally meant. So blame me not him!

My slice doesn't contain <u>all</u> the apple and blackberries that were used in the pie, but its shape and its taste mean that you know for certain that this is not an individual beef and onion pasty, and you can have a good guess at whether there will be enough for seconds!

When we preach any little bit of the Bible, that particular passage implies the whole of God's large redemptive plan. Of course, our preaching of the Bible passage must accurately explain its original meaning and purpose. We must set our word into its sentence, paragraph, chapter, book and wider Biblical theology. But when we do that, then even the very shortest exposition, or the simplest explanation, will imply the rest.

This explains several phenomena to me.

I remember a young couple that had become Christians after an extended phase of exposure to the gospel. Their Christian friend had been faithfully bringing them to our church's evangelistic events for several years. They had been stubbornly resistant. But then, after a totally surprising conversion, I sat down with them one Sunday evening for our first follow-on, Christian basics chat. They had been heavily involved in freemasonry. I knew about the freemasonry, but they didn't know that I knew. I realised that this would be a topic that we'd need to address in time, but I'd decided not to bring it up in the first conversation with them as new Christians. They arrived, and began: 'I don't know if you know that we're freemasons.' I smiled sheepishly. 'But we want you to know that now we've become Christians, if there is any issue about Christians being freemasons, we certainly intend to drop the freemasonry.' This is a topic that we'd never discussed previously. But they'd already joined the dots. 'If Jesus is who we've received Him to be and are now following, everything must come under His authority. And that includes freemasonry.'

In other words, they'd inferred some of the dimensions of the entire pie from the tiny slice they'd started to nibble!

And another phenomenon is what often happens to a preacher after preaching on a Sunday morning. In the after-church chat, someone says 'thank you for your sermon. It made me realise that I must ...' and they then talk about something that was <u>nothing</u> to do with the topic of the sermon. Why does that happen? I think it is because they have drawn conclusions about the shape of the whole pie from looking closely at just one bit ... they've realised that if this particular thing is true, then it must also have implications for that other topic that has been on their mind. It is wonderfully humbling when that happens, because we realise that the Spirit really does blow where

He wills, taking the Word of God to grow the people of God in the way He chooses.

It doesn't matter which bit of the Bible we preach, we must just preach it right. And by 'right' I mean that we must appreciate this individual bite-sized chunk in the light of the rest. And when we do that, we will be preaching the gospel and we will be preaching the kingdom and we will be preaching Jesus and we will be preaching the cross and we will be preaching discipleship.

We certainly ought to aim to help people to 'join the dots' (and this is one reason why 'application' matters in sermons). But the groundwork for any dot-joining is done in the preaching of God's whole counsel, implying the shape of the whole pie every time we preach any slice.

The 'little' implies the 'large'.

The large needs the little

Biblical theology tells the story of the whole Bible as one story, progressively revealed and focusing on God's acts of salvation in Jesus, which result in a new heavens and new earth established for His glory. Our task is to understand what any particular text means when seen in its proper relationship to this gospel[3].

Like Schubert's 'Unfinished Symphony' – which always needed the addition of one-and-a-half more movements – the story of the Old Testament always needed the finale added.

---

3   Graeme Goldsworthy, *Gospel and Wisdom* (Paternoster Press, 1987) p. 171.

Here's a second image. Imagine a 1,000-piece jigsaw. You have just managed to fit together 999 of the pieces, and the final piece is in your hand.

That remaining piece in your hand only has any meaning if it is seen as a part of the whole. If you look at it very closely, you may be able to work out that the rest of the jigsaw is probably a seascape, or a portrait, or a photo of Baked Beans. Or, more likely, it will all remain a bit unclear. But one thing is certain: there's nothing very interesting about this single piece in itself. You'd never hang it on the wall as a piece of art to be admired!

But now look back at the rest of the jigsaw. Your eyes are immediately drawn to what is missing. The gap is crying out for the last remaining piece to be found and added. Complete the picture! Once it's put in its place, the picture will make sense. The 'large' needs the 'little'.

Jesus Himself models this approach to us. Do you remember the first Easter Sunday evening? What would you do if you had just been raised from the dead?! Jesus conducts a whole Old Testament Bible overview. Walking to Emmaus with two disciples, Luke 24 is the whole Bible story told in seven miles! 'Beginning with Moses and all the Prophets, he interpreted to them in all the Scriptures the things concerning himself' (Luke 24:27). And then later that evening, He repeats the same pattern with the eleven and those who were with them. '"These are my words that I spoke to you while I was still with you, that everything written about me in the Law of Moses and the Prophets and the Psalms must be fulfilled." Then he opened their minds to understand the Scriptures' (Luke 24:44-45).

Some people interpret these verses to mean that Jesus claims every verse in the Old Testament contains some implicit reference to Him. But that's not quite what He says. The point is not that every verse is about Jesus, but rather that in every one of the three sections of the Old Testament – in the Law, and in the former/latter Prophets, and in the Writings – there are verses/passages that speak about the Messiah, and His sufferings, and His resurrection, and His welcome into glory, and the worldwide proclamation about Him.[4] Jesus 'went through the entire Scripture, front to back'[5] to point that it is all poised on tiptoe, waiting for Him. The 999 pieces of the jigsaw are crying out for the final piece to be added.

---

4   Andrew Reid, *Teaching 1 Samuel* (PT/Christian Focus, 2019).

5   Darrell L Bock, *Luke* (Baker, 1994) vol. 2 p. 1917.

I have recently been working in the book of Daniel. Commentators differ on how we should interpret the numbers in the vision that Daniel is given in chapter 9. But they agree that this greatly beloved man is told that history is made up of 'seventy sevens' (which, despite some Bible translations, are probably not literal 'weeks', but seventy 'periods of time'). My understanding is that the 'anointed one who shall be cut off' (in Dan. 9:26) is Jesus the Christ, who arrives after sixty-nine of these seventy sevens ... that is, He comes when the timeline is one 'seven' short of the whole, whilst history is still awaiting its last 'seven'. It's a similar idea to the genealogy that begins Matthew's gospel: three blocks of fourteen generations leaves us one 'seven' short of the complete seven-sevens. These are mathematical ways of saying: we need the New Testament to complete the story. No wonder Matthew begins his gospel with the story of wise men walking on stage in Matthew 2 looking for the King that the Old Testament has left us waiting for. Where is he? That's what they ask, and it's also what thoughtful readers of the Old Testament should be asking. Complete the picture!

For the Old Testament writers lead us to 'wait for the consolation of Israel', as Simeon did (in Luke 2:25-32). And the New Testament writers show us that Jesus is the Lord's Christ that we've been longing for: now 'my eyes have seen your salvation'.

Christ is presented to us as 'the end of the Law' (Rom. 10:4) – not in the sense that the Old Testament is done away with through His coming, but that He is the destination towards which it was always headed. All of the Bible is all about Him.

All the Bible writers have that kind of timeline: 999 pieces of the history jigsaw are waiting for Jesus. So, as they write for us, they teach us that is the theological approach we should adopt to understand world history. We can sometimes make it sound as if our job as readers is to get the Bible writers out of the way in order to discover the Jesus behind their writing. As if we are only being told about Mark's Jesus, or Luke's Jesus … but there is 'a real Jesus' hiding behind them for us to find. But there is no Jesus other than the one they tell us about.

Think of a superbly detailed painting by the seventeenth-century, Dutch artist, Rembrandt. 'We do not understand it by taking a photo of the "thing" that Rembrandt painted and comparing it with the painting itself'[6]. That would be ridiculous.

Our job is to concentrate on the painting by Rembrandt, not the photo. The Bible writers are the artists that God has used. The meaning of the Bible text is to be totally identified with their original intent to show us this 'long expected Jesus'. We concentrate not on 'the events' but the way that the text presents those events to us in Scripture. We are not supposed to imagine what the Bible writer may or may not have been thinking or feeling when he wrote, but to read carefully what the words actually say, for they are our only sure guide to the intention he was thinking or feeling.

---

6   John H Sailhamer, *The Meaning of the Pentateuch* (IVP, 2009) p. 19.

Their words are to determine how we are to read and understand the Bible. Every time I proclaim anything from the Bible, my presentation will always point people to Jesus, just as the Bible writers always do. Everything I say will either mention Him and His work explicitly ... or leave a huge hole that He alone can fill.

That is how John the Baptist spoke. His message was essentially: 'don't come to me, because all I can do is make you wet. Go to someone who can do the authentic Holy-Spirit-work of forgiving sins. Look over there: there's the Lamb of God who takes away the sin of the world!' Our role is to be like John the Baptist: I am not the Christ ... <u>he</u> is the bridegroom! 'He must increase, but I must decrease' (John 3:30).

This has a particular clarity as we talk about the Old Testament. Sometimes it can sound as if we're playing 'where's Wally?'[7] as we read something in the Old Testament. Is He in the fiery furnace? Is He hiding behind the lions? Is He in disguise as Daniel himself? And at its worst, when we just can't find the well-hidden Jesus anywhere in our story, we go back to bouncing the ball ... so that we 'bounce off' this story into somewhere else in the Bible that's more straightforward. The Old Testament becomes just a negative to provide a contrast to Jesus the positive, or it poses the question to which He is the answer.

This will not do!

Two better questions to ask are: how does this story-within-its-context cause me to yearn for the Jesus-who-

---

7   Or 'Where's Waldo?' in the American version!

is-to-come? and how does the coming of the Lord Jesus change the way I read this story?

That Jesus is that last piece is not self-apparent. Certain things have been hidden by God, the Lord of heaven and earth, 'from the wise and understanding and revealed to little children' (Matt. 11:25). Our minds must be opened to understand that Jesus is the subject of the whole of the Old Testament. Which is exactly what happened to those disciples on that first Easter Sunday.

But there's a bit more to say than this. The Jesus who is at the centre of the Bible and at the turning point in human history must be defined a bit more. To say that Jesus is the hermeneutical key to the Bible is too vague. Which of us would disagree? Of course we must read everything through Him. But there are just too many Jesuses. So the liberation theologian will read everything in the Bible through the lens of Jesus the fighter-for-the-rights-of-the-oppressed. The feminist through Jesus the liberator of women. The touchy-feely Christian through a Jesus who is 'more beautiful than diamonds'. The Last-Bastion-of-Truth brigade through Jesus the propositional-truth-speaker. Every clique wants to recast Jesus in their own image, as the patron saint of their own particular cause.

Who is the Jesus that the Bible writers present to us? We must make sure that our Jesus is their Jesus, for their Jesus is the only Jesus. And their Jesus is the one who 'must be lifted up' (John 3:14; 12:32-33), who came 'to give his life as a ransom for many' (Mark 10:45). The crucified Jesus. The King ... and the Cross. The structure of each of the four gospels underlines this point, by giving so much space to the events of the last week of Jesus' life. It has been suggested that a Gospel is essentially a passion narrative with an introduction[8].

From hindsight, 'after the sufferings of Christ and the subsequent glories' (1 Pet. 1:11), it all makes sense. That's the point at which it made sense to the disciples: 'when you have lifted up the Son of Man, then you will know that I am he' (John 8:28 c.f. 2:22). And similarly for the Old Testament writers, that is when it was clear 'what person or time the Spirit of Christ in (the Old Testament prophesies) was indicating' (1 Pet. 1:10-12). The cross pinpoints which Jesus is the Christ for which the Old Testament yearned.

The 'large' Old Testament story has always been needing the 'little'[9] final piece of jigsaw: 'Jesus Christ, and him crucified' (1 Cor. 2:2).

Preaching the little and preaching the large

Let's now draw the conclusion.

Any bit of the Bible (if it is understood rightly in its whole-Bible context) implies the whole: the slice implies the pie.

The whole of the Bible is waiting for Jesus, the crucified King: the jigsaw needs its final piece.

In these analogies, what <u>is</u> the pie, or the jigsaw? In very simple terms, it is what God has revealed to us about

---

8   Mark takes 444 verses to tell about three years of Jesus' life, and 240 verses to cover one week. That is slowing down the rate of story-telling by a factor of eighty-five!

9   Obviously I'm not claiming that the cross is, in itself, merely a 'little' thing!

Himself. It is His purposes and plans for this world and the next. 1 Corinthians 2 talks about this as the 'secret and hidden wisdom of God', 'what God has prepared for those who love him', 'what God has revealed', 'the thoughts of God', 'the things feely given us by God', 'the things of the Spirit of God', and 'the mind of the Lord'. And all of these things are taught to 'those who are spiritual' by the Spirit who is from God.

We only know these things because God has revealed them. And He has revealed them to us, by His Holy Spirit, in His Word. Read the Bible and you are eating the pie/ looking at the jigsaw!

When you picked up this book, you might have thought from the title that you'd be encouraged to preach topical sermons on the subject of the death of Christ. Use a concordance or a systematic theology book as an encyclopaedia, collect data from various entries, and mix it all together. Instead, the rallying cry of this book is 'preach the Bible'. The whole Bible and nothing but the Bible. If we 'preach the Bible' – and not just the texts in the Bible that specifically mention 'the cross' – if we preach <u>any</u> part of the Bible (however long or short), it will teach us what God has revealed to us about Himself, and therefore teach us about the cross.

There are many dangers in 'topical preaching'. I have been recently in a majority-Muslim country training a group of church leaders in expository preaching. They had not heard expository preaching before, since all their previous experience had been topical preaching: this week's sermon may be about 'faith', and next week will be on 'relationships'. There are several things that we said to them to try to persuade them of the value of regular, expository preaching. One of the main advantages is that God sets the agenda. In topical preaching, I choose the topics on the basis of what I think is important. But topics that I think are important may not be subjects that the Bible thinks are important. For example, I might want to preach on the subject of 'music in church'. But there are only two verses in the whole of the New Testament that are directly about that (and those two verses, Eph. 5:19 and Col. 3:16, parallel one another) ... so maybe this isn't that important a subject (even if we think it is!)? Of course, 'putting on kindness, humility, meekness and patience, bearing with one another in love' may have lots of implications for how we do music in church, but I guess that none of those instructions would appear in my word search for 'music'.

Obviously 'the cross' is a topic that the Bible <u>does</u> think important!

Going through the Bible in an orderly way, aiming simply to understand what each bit means in its own context, forces us to speak about the topics that God thinks are important, in the ways that He determines, and as often as He choses, and with the appropriate levels of repetition and emphasis that He decides. In His wisdom, He chose <u>not</u> to give us His revelation in the form of an encyclopaedia of topics.

There is no entry entitled 'the cross'. Everything that the Bible tells us about the cross comes to us with its own perspective, setting and context.

Expository preaching also means that we will be edgy! By definition, a topical sermon tells people what I already know about that topic. Preaching 'the next bit of the Bible' forces me to consider things that I may not have considered, let alone understood. It's far more risky. I don't know where this passage might take me.

For example, I was recently preaching through Titus. I'm not sure I would have said that the grace of God that has come to us 'saves us' <u>and</u> 'trains us' – putting those two things together – if 2:11-14 hadn't put them together. Or in 3:4-8, it is a real surprise to see that 'the washing of regeneration' and 'renewal by the Holy Spirit' are brought together at our salvation: I probably would have thought of those as two separate topics, and thereby, like much contemporary Christian understanding, divided the work of Jesus from the work of the Spirit. Expository preaching will surprise the preacher, and the congregation.

So, of course, preparing for expository preaching will be far better for the spiritual health of the preacher, because I will be learning new things week after week, as I discover what God says, and not repeating what I think I would have said anyway.

But to come back to the main point: this book is not written to encourage more topical sermons about 'the cross'. The Proclamation Trust exists to encourage expository preaching: tell us what God says in the way that God says it as often as God says it and with the interpretation that God gives us in the Bible for everything He says. In describing why he has given his life to always preaching expository sermons like this, John MacArthur says this:

'If you don't have the *meaning* of Scripture, you do not have the Word of God at all. If you miss the true sense of what God has said, you are not actually preaching God's Word! That reality has compelled me for nearly forty years of preaching.'[10] We want to preach sermons that don't merely use the Bible the way that a drunk man uses a lamp post ... for support![11] Rather than leaning on the Bible, we want to stand directly under the Bible. We want to let the Bible be front-and-centre in everything we say: 'come and see what this bit of the Bible says to us'.

But remember: we are not just talking about 'giving sermons'. By 'preaching', we're meaning the work of all Christians to speak of the Lord Jesus Christ to the world (of which, appointed ministers giving sermons in church is one subset).

Any Christian can take any bit of the Bible, set it into its sentence, paragraph, chapter, book and wider Biblical theology. And then trust this bit of the Bible. I don't need to bring in a whole lot of other bits from elsewhere to complete something that is otherwise inadequate. The rest is implied. And that implied remainder will have the cross at its very heart.

Our task is to proclaim the pie, slice by slice. To fit the last piece of the whole Bible jigsaw.

BUT ... let me ask a genuine question in a slightly outrageous way: does the Bible preach the cross enough? I know that some people will feel that, if I only preach

---

10   'Why I still preach the Bible' in *Preaching the Cross* (Crossway, 2007) p. 139.

11   David Helm, *Expositional Preaching* (Crossway, 2014) p. 24.

'the next bit of the Bible' in an expository way, I won't preach the gospel often enough or clearly enough for non-Christians to be converted.

There is an article currently being re-circulated on Twitter that advises caution over expository preaching as a method. In particular, the author argues, it is not 'the best fit for evangelistic preaching' because 'there are *particular truths* most adapted to speak to non-Christians (witness our Lord's example) and that it is these truths, and the texts that best epitomize them, which have special and regular prominence in most effective evangelistic ministries. The men most used in the conversion of sinners in the past have known what these texts are.'[12]

One way in which this objection is expressed is in the old division of the Sunday services – in the morning, we hold the 'teaching' service, and the evening we hold the 'gospel' service. Similarly, many churches hold regular 'guest services' as the best place to bring along your non-Christian friend because we intend to 'preach the gospel' there. Which is a strange thing to say: are we admitting that we don't preach the gospel when we preach the Bible on every other Sunday? Really?!

I think it is a mistake to seek to reduce the gospel to 'an irreducible minimum'. It would seem arbitrary – and slightly ridiculous – to think that there is some kind of 'canon within a canon', a list of particular 'gospel' phrases where the <u>real</u> power of God resides in a more concentrated form than in the rather less-powerful residue of the Bible. And

---

12   Iain H. Murray, 'Expository Preaching' – Time for Caution (accessed on The Banner of Truth website, dated 18 June 2010).

those particular words must be verbalised, in some kind of tick-box exercise, if someone is to become a Christian.

The evidence from the gospels and from Acts is that the content of apostolic preaching is much bigger than that. Even if it can be condensed into concise summaries, it is all Tardis-like – much bigger on the inside, with an infinite number of rooms, corridors and storage spaces, implying a huge Biblical theology.

Our job is to say what God says, and let Him preach the cross – His all-ages-long plan of salvation – through any and every passage in the Bible.

For, if I preach the 'little', I will preach that 'large' plan of God. And if I preach the 'large' plan of God, I will preach its centre at the cross of Christ.

5
SOME IMPLICATIONS

Trust the Word

In Chapter 3, we considered the powerful effectiveness of God's word. It is inconceivable that God could say something and His words be left hanging in the ether, or 'return empty' to Him: 'it shall accomplish that which I purpose' (Isa. 55:10-11).

I've been praying that every Christian reading this book will be strengthened in their conviction that if the Word of God is proclaimed then God will do things. It is not the preserve of special people to do the proclaiming, for God has commissioned and equipped every Christian. It is not that there are special places where the Word of God is more potent, for the power is in the Word not the place. It is not that there is a particular format for the proclamation that will be more successful, for it is God's work not our 'wisdom' (1 Cor. 2:5).

When is the 'power' control turned full on? Simply when the unbound Word of God is 'preached' (2 Tim. 2:8-10).

Standing alongside Ezekiel in his valley of lost hope, it is difficult for the wannabe preacher to hold onto this conviction. Can these bones live?! But Jesus anticipates this feeling in us and tells His disciples the stories of Mark 4. In three stories (verses 3-9, 26-28 and 30-32),

Jesus speaks of a seed being sown: this seed is 'the word of God' (14). And each story ends with the same result: a huge harvest (8, 27b-28 and 32). One of the reasons for these stories is that Jesus is teaching His disciples why preaching is His priority. The reason is simply that it is effective. Any harvest there is going to be will come this way: the seed must be put in the ground! But of course we face things that cause us to doubt its effectiveness. The first challenge is **wastage**. In the first story, three quarters of the sown seed comes to nothing. It may be immediately snatched away, or only temporarily effective until persecution or worldliness choke it. So much seed-sowing does <u>not</u> produce a harvest. The challenge in the second story is **delay**. The farmer puts seed in the ground, and when he gets up the next morning and checks the field, there is nothing to show. And it's the same on the following day. And day after day for months. Nothing! In the third story, it is the apparent **insignificance** of the seed: it looks highly unlikely that something so tiny could do <u>anything</u>, let alone produce the biggest garden tree!

Of course this is how we feel with the Word of God in our mouths. We feel as optimistic as Ezekiel prophesying to bones! If I speak this, will it really be powerful? It seems unlikely. And when I do speak it, my fears are realized: nothing much seems to happen, and so much of it never produces anything. My conviction is undermined.

But ...

This is the very reason for this teaching from Jesus: there will be a massive harvest. The Word of God will do it. Thirtyfold and sixtyfold and a hundredfold. Trust this Word.

Preach the Word

The danger of a book entitled 'Preaching the Cross' is that bookshop-browsers think its message is for professional sermonisers. And now I'm shooting myself in the foot with a section entitled 'preach the Word': yes, those people whose job is giving sermons should definitely give sermons on the cross.

But this call to arms is for all Christians. When we became Christians, we became prophets (as we saw in Chapter 1). And if the Lord God has spoken – if the lion has roared – who can but prophesy (Amos 3:8)? If He has spoken, then we have to speak. Let's all 'preach the Word'.

And this is nothing more complicated than opening the Bible and speaking it out. Indeed, it can and should be done in lots of situations – whenever and wherever appropriate. One-to-one, or one-to-many ... the numbers are not the point. The Bible's logic is 'all' to 'all' ... all Christians can prophesy so that all can be saved.

And what we should proclaim is what the Bible says. Of course, we must set this particular word into its sentence, paragraph, chapter, book and wider Biblical theology. We must let the pastoral purpose of the original author control our understanding. We must let the Bible writers' theological timeline take us to Jesus. And when we do that, however simple or short our exposition, we will be preachers of the Word.

There are lots of good resources available to equip Christians to read the Bible like this with their friends and colleagues. But never let those things mislead us about where the power of God resides: it's in His Word. The resources are one means God uses ... and me speaking truth is another means God uses ... for He uses all kinds of different means so that His powerful Word is heard.

For those who feel ill-equipped to do this, there are lots of training courses that can help with Bible-handling skills. But actually, of course, the best equipping will come from sitting under the Word ourselves, and personally experiencing this powerful Word of God at work in us, to change and train us. The ascended Lord Jesus has given pastor-teachers to His church to 'equip the saints for the work of ministry ... (of) speaking the truth in love' (Eph. 4:12, 15) ... that is, to equip all of us to be 'preachers'!

Just don't professionalise the task: God has made us preachers of His Word. All of us. Preach it!

Preach the cross

I heard of a coffee queue conversation between a group of theological educators at a conference on the book of Romans. One college lecturer asked another how many of his students were now engaged in international mission. 'Oh, we're a theological college, not a missionary college' was the reply. What a terrible indictment of the theology they were teaching. If it didn't lead to proclamation to the world, then I'd suggest that very little understanding was being achieved, not least of the book of Romans!

We must always ask the significance of any part of the Bible. What is the significance of 'the cross' for the world, the church, our neighbour, our friend ...? The death of Jesus is 'for the nation ... (and) also to gather into one the children of God who are scattered abroad' (John 11:52). God our Saviour 'desires all people to be saved and to come to a knowledge of the truth' which is why 'the man, Christ Jesus ... gave himself as a ransom for all' (1 Tim. 2:3-6).

So 'the word of the cross' is the message of the powerful Word of God that everyone needs to hear. It is for the entire planet. This gospel is public truth. It's not something for certain personality types who are 'into this kind of thing'. It's not to be targeted at one ethnic group, or a particular class. It's never inappropriate for anyone anywhere.

God Himself has arrived on the world stage as King. This momentous event in world history changes everything for everyone. For now, in the last moments of history, we have a very limited time to call on the name of the Lord Jesus so we are safe on the Day of Wrath.

There is a tone that is appropriate for such a proclamation. For sure, it needs to be urgent, with pleading and persuading. It will come with confidence and zeal and boldness. We are heralds who publish this startling news to the world: the risen Jesus Christ is Lord!

Get out there and preach the cross!

6
PREACHING THE CROSS

It's all very well making the case for 'preaching the cross' by 'preaching the Bible' ... and (at the same time) for 'preaching the Bible' as the way to be 'preaching the cross'. But what does that look like in practice?

This chapter gives a series of worked examples. Each case attempts to embed the text into its immediate context and into wider Biblical theology. And, each exposition is driven by the firm belief that a preacher doesn't need to say everything to be saying enough.

Genesis 22:1-18

This is a tantalising story: it seems to be SO blatantly pointing ahead to the cross. Just consider a phrase like 'your son, your only son, whom you love' (2). Picture the wood 'laid on' the son who carries it up the hill to the place of sacrifice (cf John 19:17). It's such an obvious picture of 'substitution', as a ram (shame it's not a lamb!) is provided. It is very tempting to allegorise the whole thing and to search for Jesus in every thicket.

But the New Testament doesn't make that connection explicitly. Instead, it zooms into the <u>faith</u> of Abraham. James 2:21-23 says that the story shows Abraham was justified by works (!), and Hebrews 11:17-19 says the story gives a model of what faith does – being sure that God would keep His promises.

The key thing is to place this incident into the larger jigsaw. Genesis 3-11 has graphically depicted the spread of rebellion and death: 'the earth is filled ...' not just with people (Gen. 1:28) but now also with the violence (6:11, 13) they bring. Humankind are not in the Garden of Eden – that secure place of delights – but in the place of terrible 'curse'. God's solution is to promise 'blessing' that will come through an offspring' (12:1-3; 15:1-6; 17:1-14). Of course the New Testament calls this 'the gospel announced in advance' (see Gal. 3:8, NIV), for what God says to Abraham is nothing less than the promise of salvation. That's the context for Genesis 22.

So, back in our story, there are three key moments, or turning points:

v2 the extraordinary command of God. Of course this instruction is all the more extraordinary because it comes only one chapter after the birth of the long-awaited Isaac (21:1-7) and the moment where God's promise of offspring is, for the first time, made specific to the son named Isaac (21:12b). The promised blessing is finally being realised. So what is endangered by God's command is not just Abraham's family line, but the blessing of the world: Abraham is to slay the means of salvation that God said He would supply! So this verse sets up the tension between the promise of God and the command of God.

v8 the faith of Abraham. Abraham is confident that, whatever happens, God will keep His promises. He is sure that if Isaac is the promised one and yet is killed, God would bring Isaac back from the dead in order to be true to His Word (Heb. 11:19 and cf Rom. 4:17 too): God will save the world! Nothing can thwart the promise of God.

v14 the place-naming (usually a big clue towards 'the point' of a story), looks forward to a <u>future</u> provision by God of whatever is needed so that His promises are kept. Of course this forward-looking faith anticipates the sacrificial system: sacrifices will be provided 'on this mountain' (that is, in Moriah a place which is only mentioned twice in the Old Testament: here in verse 1, and then in 2 Chronicles 3:1 as the site for the temple in Jerusalem). Immediately after this place-naming, the covenant promise is reiterated and God secures it by His oath (16) – the same oath that is fulfilled in Jesus (Luke 1:73) so that 'we might have strong encouragement to hold fast to the hope set before us' (Heb. 6:13-18).

This 'chunks' the passage into three scenes linked to these three moments:

- God tests Abraham
- Abraham trusts God
- 'The Lord will provide'

And these three might produce a Theme Sentence for the passage that goes something like this:

Abraham trusts that the Lord will provide whatever is needed to save the world.

If I preach this passage like this, with this Big Picture Biblical theology, will I be 'preaching the cross'? Yes, indeed ... AND without needing to allegorise the entire story as a scene set at Calvary. I can be confident that I will proclaim that:

- the all-time salvation purpose of God is to bring about blessing (instead of cursings) for the world and He will provide it;

- nothing will stop Him providing that salvation, even if it requires Him to raise someone from the dead in order to achieve it;

- sacrifice is important in this ... not some child-sacrifice in 2,000 BC, nor a series of animal sacrifices to be carried out in a Jewish temple at this same location in the following centuries, but through the sacrifice of a much-loved only Son;

- God solemnly promises that He will keep this promise, and His unchangeable purpose provides a sure and steadfast anchor for us. I can be sure of my salvation because God has promised it, and promised it with an oath.

Daniel 2:1-49

This chapter may not seem to have very much to do with 'preaching the cross'. But it is all about the eternal kingdom that God will establish, and, as we've seen, that is the gospel.

The first thing to decide about this chapter is its structure. It does suggest a chiasm (building to a midpoint, with the second half of the passage mirroring the first). The centre point is verse 19a where 'the mystery (of Nebuchadnezzar's dream) is revealed' to Daniel. And this is significant because there is a running theme about the inability both of the king's magicians to tell the king his dreams (10), and also of 'the gods' because 'their dwelling is not with flesh' (11). In sharp contrast, Daniel's God 'reveals deep and hidden things' (22). It might seem that the key truth of the passage therefore is <u>that</u> God reveals.

However, although we don't get to the retelling of the dream and its interpretation until verse 31, <u>what</u> God reveals is where the story takes us in the second half of the chapter (in verses 31-35, interpreted in verses 36-45). So whilst the story turns on the fact <u>that</u> God reveals, the point of the story is <u>what</u> He reveals.

This links with the broader purpose of the book: God is revealing to His people 'another reality', which we might describe as 'what is happening in the heavenlies'. And God's people need to know this to live in the world we <u>can</u> see whilst holding firm to the reality of the world we <u>can't</u> see. The way to live in exile, as we groan, wanting to be 'at home with the Lord' is to live not just 'by sight' but 'by faith' (cf 2 Cor. 5:6-7). And this is the message not merely for Daniel and his contemporaries in their literal exile in Babylon, but also for God's people after their return from exile in Babylon.[1] It is the same message

---

1   On the basis of Daniel 1:21 we can be sure that the first readers were after Cyrus' decree that enabled the return to Jerusalem. They would therefore read the book of Daniel after the exile was

for God's people today who still live 'as sojourners and
exiles' waiting for our inheritance 'kept in heaven for you'
(1 Pet. 2:11, 1:3-5). Living like this is what it means to be
'wise'.

So we need to know what Nebuchadnezzar is told in
his dream.

My three headings for this chapter are:

- the God who reveals ...

- ... that kingdoms come and go

- ... that He will set up His forever-kingdom.

This enables lots of opportunity for good story-telling,
which is so important when explaining truth from any
part of Old Testament narrative. But it also firmly puts the
emphasis on <u>what</u> God reveals through the dream and its
interpretation.

God revealed to Nebuchadnezzar the heavenly view
of reality. For sure, God acknowledges the might of this
'king of kings, to whom the God of heaven has given
the kingdom, the power, the might and the glory' (37) –
extraordinarily exalted language for a pagan ruler! And
astonishingly it is God who gave this position to him. But
God sees all the impressive kingdoms of this world as here
today, gone tomorrow. I was preaching from this Bible
book recently at a conference in Greece. It was quite a
moment to be speaking about the great kingdoms of the
past – Babylon, Persia, Greece, Rome – surrounded by
ruins left by the now-defunct powerful Hellenistic Empire.

over, still needing to learn the lessons from the exile to equip them
for their life back home.

It had all gone. It may be very obvious from hindsight, but it is much harder to believe when you are living in such a kingdom, with all its symbols of power and might.

The Big Idea of the chapter, for people seeing such symbols, is that *God will set up a kingdom that will break in pieces all those other kingdoms and then itself stand forever, never to be destroyed.*

Here is the gospel of the kingdom that Jesus and the New Testament preaches: the eternal reign of 'the stone' that became a great mountain and filled the whole earth. For God has given to Jesus the only name that will outlast time, the name superior, better and triumphant over every other name, a name before which every knee will bow. He is not just King Jesus, but the King of Kings. No, even greater than that, He is the Lord over all other kings. This Jesus that will reign is (in Dale Ralph Davis' inimitable description) the carpenter who makes coffins for kingdoms!

Here is a very good example of the way in which 'the large needs the little': the big picture of human history that God gives to Nebuchadnezzar was always waiting for the last piece of the jigsaw, to know the identity of this stone not made by human hands. Now we see the promised Christ the King, the 'stone that the builders rejected', who is the one that 'has become the cornerstone' (Mark 12:10). His rejection and His exaltation – both parts of the gospel story – are indeed 'the Lord's doing': it is a 'marvelous' thing to see that the cross (that encapsulates His rejection) has become the underpinning for the building of His eternal kingdom.

Mark 10:45

This climactic verse in Mark's gospel seems like a far more obvious text for 'preaching the cross'. How many times have we heard sermons on this verse that take us to the slave market (or the pawn brokers) to describe what a 'ransom' is: Jesus paid the price to buy our freedom from slavery! The danger of such easy short-cuts is that we end up preaching a slave market analogy rather than what the text actually says. I've chosen this as another of our worked examples because it's a place where tighter exegesis proves invaluable.

This verse is like a missing piece in the jigsaw of the gospel that Mark preaches. Throughout his book, he has been assembling multiple pieces of evidence for three major themes:

- Jesus is the Redeemer. After the story of Jesus feeding crowds in the desert and then walking on water, Mark adds his editorial comment to explain why the disciples are 'utterly astounded': 'they did not understand about the loaves, but their hearts were hardened' (6:52). The feeding miracle is the only miracle that occurs in all four gospels, and it comes twice in Mark ... and, as if to make the repetition even more significant, Mark now says that there's something so explanatory about this miracle that the disciples should not have found water-walking unusual! I think the point is that Jesus is self-consciously referring back to Israel's Exodus from Egypt, as 'I am' walks across water as if on dry ground, and provides bread from heaven for hungry, breadless people in the wilderness. Towards the end of the Old Testament period, the prophets had predicted that God would come to save His people from exile, and His rescue then would be just like this. There was going to be a re-run of that first Exodus: rescue from captivity in a foreign land (Isa. 48:20), with a way (40:3-4) though a desert (43:19) and through sea (43:16; 44:27), with water provided en route (43:20; 48:21), and with God Himself in front and behind to protect (52:12). No wonder Isaiah's favourite name for the Lord is his Exodus-name, 'the Redeemer'. In Mark 6, we are given lots of heavy hints that Jesus is claiming to be that one-and-only Redeemer God doing the second Exodus that Isaiah (and other prophets) predicted.

- I am a sinner and I cannot save myself. Many stories in Mark's gospel explain our hopeless state. Evil comes out from somewhere deep inside each of us, rather than being something that infects us from the outside (7:20-23). Sin takes us to hell, and hell is so awful it's better to cut off a limb than go there (9:42-48). But since we can't cut out our own heart (!), it is impossible for us to inherit eternal life, or get ourselves into the kingdom of God, or to be saved (10:17-31). Like the Syrophoenician woman, we are the foreign 'dogs' who have no right to expect help (7:24-30). And, what's worse, we lack even basic understanding of all of this (8:14-21) unless our eyes are miraculously opened. How helpless we are.

- Jesus must die. This is the sombre drumbeat through the second half of the gospel. He doesn't just predict that He <u>will</u> die, but three-times repeats His conviction that He <u>must</u> be delivered over to be condemned, to be mocked, flogged and crucified, for that is why He came (8:31; 9:31; 10:33).

Three themes. But only at 10:45 are we told how they fit together. Only now do we get the final piece of a jigsaw. Jesus the Redeemer must die as a ransom for us, for we cannot give enough to save our own soul (8:37). It is the death of Jesus – as He drinks the cup of God's wrath and is overwhelmed in the waters of judgement (10:38-39) – that is the ransom, the price of our redemption. Jesus will lose His life in this world in order that we might gain life in the world to come (8:34-38).

It's almost impossible to do justice to what this verse is telling us unless it is kept firmly set within its whole-gospel context. This verse provides the answer to bubbling questions about Jesus – who He is and what He thinks He is doing. Without insisting on that context, we will probably lose all the Exodus allusions that come from that word 'ransom', and almost certainly our over-simplistic attempts to explain the cross will end up getting it wrong!

1 Thessalonians 1:9-10

After just three weeks preaching in Thessalonica, Paul is expelled from the city (Acts 17:1-9) and the region (Acts 17:10-15). There are, of course, lots of books today about church planting, but I've not found one that suggests this strategy: go to a place for three weeks and then leave! No wonder Paul is worried how this young church is faring.

He gets as far as Athens and sends back a friend to find out if they have kept going as Christians. Now Timothy has returned to Athens with the news that, yes, they are 'standing fast' (1 Thess. 3:8). And Paul is so relieved, he immediately picks up his pen and writes to them.

Chapter 1 of the letter is filled with his thanksgiving for them: this rag-bag group of uninstructed, immature Christians are 'the church in God' (1:1). He can be confident of this, and confident that God 'has chosen you' (1:4) because he can see evidence of God's work in them. And chapter 1 lists that evidence.

First, Paul remembers their faith, love and hope (1:3), that familiar New Testament shorthand for a genuine Christian, which is made visible in their work, labour and steadfastness. He can see it.

Then, secondly, he remembers that they 'received the word in much affliction' (6-8). In this, they imitated both Paul and Jesus Himself: difficulty and hardship didn't stop them. And they wouldn't have become Christians in circumstances like that unless God was at work. Clearly, He had been.

The third bit of evidence is in verses 9-10. They turned around. When Paul proclaimed Jesus in Thessalonica, the mob who set the city into an uproar (Acts 17:5) – translated in an older version as 'certain lewd fellows of the baser sort' (!) – say that Paul was preaching that 'there is another king, Jesus' (7). Of course, that is a good part of what 'Christ' means, that Jesus is a King big enough to rival the Caesar. When the Thessalonians received the gospel message, Paul notes that their whole lives were upturned to make this King their king. They started **working** for the King, serving the living and true God, and they lived their lives **waiting** for the King who'll return to deliver us from God's judgement (10).

There are different kinds of 'waiting' of course. Waiting for a bus that never turns up is very different from a child waiting for Christmas. But, for the Bible, **waiting** means **working**. In Mark 13:32-37, Jesus said that the Christian life is like a man going away, leaving his house to be looked after by his servants. We serve an absent King. Each of us is given a job to do until the time when He returns. And we are to be ready for that moment. If we are really watching out for the master, we will show that we are ready by getting on with our assigned task.

We have a family game where someone shuts their eyes to count whilst everyone else hides. When the count reaches fifty, the task is for everyone to get back to the base without being caught. The chase begins as the counter shouts: 'ready or not, here I come'. At the next coming of the Lord Jesus, when He comes riding on the clouds with great power and glory, the cry will be heard: 'ready or not, here I come'. Those who are ready and waiting will look up from their Christian service, recognise that it's Jesus their deliverer who is coming and then return to carry on with what they're already doing! We will be waiting by working. That is what repentance looks like: it's a complete U-turn from anything else to serve the King, recognising that He is the King for whom we work and wait. And that's something to do once-and-for-all, <u>and</u> every day.

Paul is confident that when we see Christians who keep going like this, then we can be sure of God's choosing. He ties together election and perseverance. Here again is the gospel.

Proclaiming 1 Thessalonians 1:9-10 will mean that we announce:

- Jesus is the King;
- repent because Jesus is the King;
- work for and wait for the King.

And how familiar is that list alongside the themes we've already identified (in Chapter 2) in the gospel presentations of the early church!

2 Timothy 2:8

Paul is encouraging his protégé Timothy to entrust the gospel to 'faithful men who will be able to teach others also' (2 Tim 2:2). Just as Paul taught him, so he is to pass on the baton. The gospel is preserved into the next generation not by locking it away, but by putting it to work. Of course the vital question is: what does such a 'faithful' person look like? And in that context, in verse 8, Paul tells Timothy to 'remember Jesus Christ, risen from the dead, the offspring of David, as preached in my gospel'.

This sounds like more familiar 'gospel' territory. Except ... where is the cross?!

Some have suggested that if the Jesus Christ that Timothy is to remember is 'risen from the dead' that must imply His preceding death (otherwise He could not be raised): so Paul really means 'remember Jesus Christ who died and then was subsequently raised from the dead ...'. Others might do a 'bouncing ball' off this verse to Romans 1:3-4 because Paul's logic here seems to be similar: Jesus' family tree shows He's a son of David and His resurrection shows He's the Son of David – that is, the Messiah. This is certainly a helpful cross-reference. But is that exactly the point that Paul is making here?

This remembering is part of a sequence of examples that Paul gives. And these examples set out two themes that run through a longer passage (2:3-13), just as they run throughout the letter:

- perseverance (to the end)
- promise (of reward at the end).

Those two themes fit with the three pictures of soldier, athlete and farmer (2:4-6). All three must **persevere** (by keeping going in obeying their commanding officer, training strenuously and always working hard in their field) for the **promised** reward (of the CO's commendation, the medal and the harvest).

Similarly in verses 8-9, Paul **perseveres** in preaching the 'gospel-for-which-I-am-suffering'. And he does this because of the **promise** of resurrection: Jesus' resurrection proves that the gospel does indeed abolish death, and bring life and immortality to light (1:10). But this life is 'the promise of life' (1:1) in contrast to what we might call 'the already gospel' of Hymenaeus, Philetus and others (2:18): their gospel has no 'promise'.

It's the same pattern in verse 10. Again, we're told that Paul **perseveres**, enduring everything. Why? So that other Christians (rather than himself) will obtain salvation. If he doesn't stick at gospel ministry, how will people finally be saved? And if Timothy doesn't stick at gospel ministry, how will people finally be saved? Persevere because of the **promise** of <u>their</u> future salvation.

And the 'faithful saying' reflects the same concerns for these 'faithful' ministers of the future. What is the Christian life like? The first half of each phrase tells us that it's dying with Jesus, enduring with Jesus, not denying Jesus and not being faithless. These four things could be taken as Paul spelling out what kind of hardship or suffering (3) he has in mind: it's all about **perseverance**. The second half of each phrase describes the horizon in our Christian life. It's the perspective – or the **promise** – of eternity: living with Jesus and reigning with Jesus (and the terrifying alternative of deniers being denied by Jesus).

Of course the perspective of the other teachers in Ephesus is something entirely different. Their horizon isn't that far sighted, future resurrection (18). Only if you have Paul's gospel perspective, only then will you endure hardship now: **perseverance** depends on understanding the **promise**.

Here then is the gospel (2:8) and the gospel 'pattern' (1:13) that Timothy is to remember and to follow. The kind of 'faithful' person in whom Timothy should invest is somebody who shows this kind of **perseverance** because they firmly believe the **promise**.

This briefest of references to the gospel here in 2 Timothy 2:8 is a 'slice' that perfectly delineates the shape of the whole pie. To preach this message from this verse is to preach the gospel of the Lord Jesus. For what is the life of Jesus apart from these very two things? As Hebrews 12:2 tells us, He 'endured the cross, despising the shame' (= perseverance) 'for the joy that was set before him ... seated at the right hand of the throne of God' (= promise).

This verse doesn't require us to bounce away to 'something else that must be in Paul's mind that he doesn't mention here'! For here, in this verse, the gospel that Paul preached and that Timothy is to remember implies the entire pie. Here is the gospel pattern. The 'faithful' person, or 'person of faith', or even 'believer', will not have their faith upset by alternative gospels. Instead they will follow their Master, and the apostle (and, for that matter, the ages-long tradition of faithful sufferers), and

- persevere (to the end)

- holding firm to the gospel promise (of reward at the end).

ABOUT THE PROCLAMATION TRUST

The Proclamation Trust is all about unashamedly preaching and teaching God's Word the Bible. Our firm conviction is that when God's Word is taught, God's voice is heard, and therefore our entire work is about helping people engage in this life transforming work.

We have three strands to our ministry:

Firstly we run the Cornhill Training Course which is a three year, part-time course to train people to handle and communicate God's Word rightly.

Secondly we have a wide portfolio of conferences we run to equip, enthuse and energise senior pastors, assistant pastors, students, ministry wives, women in ministry and church members in the work God has called them to. We also run the Evangelical Ministry Assembly each summer in London which is a gathering of over a thousand church leaders from across the UK and from around the world.

Thirdly we produce an array of resources, of which this book in your hand is one, to assist people in preaching, teaching and understanding the Bible.

For more information please go to www.proctrust.org.uk

OTHER BOOKS IN THE GET PREACHING SERIES

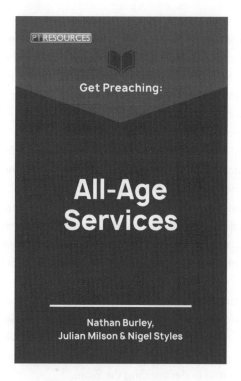

PT RESOURCES

Get Preaching:

All-Age
Services

Nathan Burley,
Julian Milson & Nigel Styles

ISBN: 978-1-5271-0383-2

Get Preaching: All-Age Services
Nathan Burley, Julian Milson & Nigel Styles

- Biblical explanation for why all-age services are important
- Practical tips for putting together an all-age service
- Part of the Get Preaching series

The church is an all-age family, and the whole family can grow through hearing the word of God preached. With the Bible at the centre of every service, Nathan Burley, Julian Milson and Nigel Styles give helpful foundations and suggestions for how to include everyone in the church family in the message, before going through a large number of worked examples.

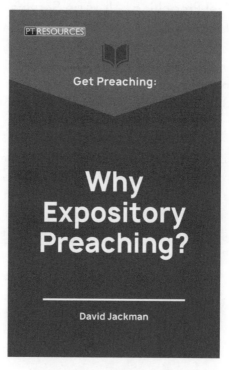

PT RESOURCES

Get Preaching:

Why Expository Preaching?

David Jackman

ISBN: 978-1-5271-0385-6

Get Preaching: Why Expository Preaching
David Jackman

- Part of the Get Preaching series
- Examines the importance of expository preaching
- Helpful suggestions for putting it into practise

At its simplest expository preaching is preaching which allows the Biblical text to direct the contents of the message, by which the church grows and flourishes.

But why is it so important?

In this short book David Jackman explains the motivation behind this method of preaching, gives instruction for putting it into practise, and works through a couple of examples of expository sermons. This book will be a crucial tool for anyone engaged in teaching God's flock.

AVAILABLE IN THE *TEACHING THE BIBLE* SERIES

ISBN 978-1-5271-0335-1

Teaching Joshua
From Text to Message
Doug Johnson

- Text–based study of the book of Joshua
- Part of the 'Teaching' series
- Great for preachers & Bible study leaders

The book of Joshua is an epic. Conquest, battles, scandal, tribalism, deceit, land registration and farewell speeches all make up this remarkable narrative. However behind all the twists and turns, highs and lows is the God who makes and keeps promises. The book of Joshua is profoundly relevant for today and needs to be declared faithfully in its entirety. To be repeatedly reminded through the pages of Joshua that God is faithful to his promises and sovereign over his people, guiding them by his powerful word to his promised rest, is truth we must never tire of hearing.

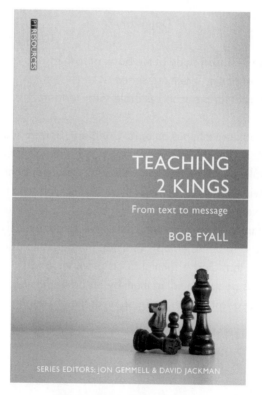

PT RESOURCES

TEACHING
2 KINGS

From text to message

BOB FYALL

SERIES EDITORS: JON GEMMELL & DAVID JACKMAN

ISBN: 978-1-5271-0157-9

Teaching 2 Kings
From Text to Message
Bob Fyall

2 Kings begins with the succession of Elijah by Elisha and flows largely downward right up to the exile of Judah in Babylon. Amidst the numerous kings and serious failings there are always the vital signs that the true God is still on the throne and working out his purposes in his people and beyond.

Like many other books containing Old Testament narrative, 1 and 2 Kings are both well-known and obscure. Certain stories are very familiar, others seldom preached or taught. It is our hope that this book will greatly help many people dig deeply into this epic narrative and serve people well by teaching it faithfully, relevantly and thoroughly.

Teaching 1 and 2 Kings (of which this is the second volume of two) is an important contribution to our 'Teaching the Bible' series. Bob's guiding hand will be of great assistance to anyone seeking to understand the familiar passages better and explore the lesser known stories well.

Christian Focus Publications

Our mission statement —

STAYING FAITHFUL

In dependence upon God we seek to impact the world through literature faithful to His infallible Word, the Bible. Our aim is to ensure that the Lord Jesus Christ is presented as the only hope to obtain forgiveness of sin, live a useful life and look forward to heaven with Him.

Our books are published in four imprints:

CHRISTIAN
FOCUS

Popular works including biographies, commentaries, basic doctrine and Christian living.

CHRISTIAN
HERITAGE

Books representing some of the best material from the rich heritage of the church.

MENTOR

Books written at a level suitable for Bible College and seminary students, pastors, and other serious readers. The imprint includes commentaries, doctrinal studies, examination of current issues and church history.

CF4•K

Children's books for quality Bible teaching and for all age groups: Sunday school curriculum, puzzle and activity books; personal and family devotional titles, biographies and inspirational stories — because you are never too young to know Jesus!

Christian Focus Publications Ltd,
Geanies House, Fearn, Ross-shire,
IV20 1TW, Scotland, United Kingdom.
www.christianfocus.com
blog.christianfocus.com